The Art of the Start

Also by Guy Kawasaki

Database 101

Hindsights

How to Drive Your Competition Crazy

Rules for the Revolutionaries

Selling the Dream

The Computer Curmudgeon

The Macintosh Way

THE ART OF THE START

THE TIME-TESTED, BATTLE-HARDENED GUIDE FOR ANYONE STARTING ANYTHING

Guy Kawasaki

PORTFOLIO

PORTFOLIO
Published by the Penguin Group
Penguin Group (USA) Inc., 375 Hudson Street, New York, New York 10014, U.S.A.
Penguin Group (Canada), 10 Alcorn Avenue, Toronto, Ontario, Canada M4V 3B2
(a division of Pearson Penguin Canada Inc.)
Penguin Books Ltd, 80 Strand, London WC2R 0RL, England
Penguin Ireland, 25 St Stephen's Green, Dublin 2, Ireland (a division of Penguin Books Ltd)
Penguin Books Australia Ltd, 250 Camberwell Road, Camberwell, Victoria 3124,
Australia (a division of Pearson Australia Group Pty Ltd)
Penguin Books India Pvt Ltd, 11 Community Centre, Panchsheel Park, New Delhi –
110 017, India
Penguin Group (NZ), Cnr Airborne and Rosedale Roads, Albany, Auckland,
New Zealand (a division of Pearson New Zealand Ltd)
Penguin Books (South Africa) (Pty) Ltd, 24 Sturdee Avenue, Rosebank, Johannesburg
2196, South Africa

Penguin Books Ltd, Registered Offices:
80 Strand, London WC2R 0RL, England

First published in 2004 by Portfolio,
a member of Penguin Group (USA) Inc.

10   9   8   7   6   5   4   3   2

Publisher's Note
This publication is designed to provide accurate and authoritative information in regard to
the subject matter covered. It is sold with the understanding that the publisher is not en-
gaged in rendering legal, accounting, or other professional services. If you require legal advice or other expert assistance, you should seek the services of a competent professional.

LIBRARY OF CONGRESS CATALOGING-IN-PUBLICATION DATA

Kawasaki, Guy, 1954–
    The art of the start : the time-tested, battle-hardened guide for anyone starting
    anything / Guy Kawasaki.
    p.   cm.
    Includes bibliographical references and index.
    ISBN 1-59184-056-2
    Special Market ISBN 1-59184-115-1   Not for resale
    1. New business enterprises.   2. Entrepreneurship.   I. Title.

HD62.5.K38 2004   658.1'1—dc22   2004044773

This book is printed on acid-free paper. ∞

Printed in the United States of America
Set in Sabon
Designed by BTD NYC

Many years ago Rudyard Kipling gave an address at McGill University in Montreal. He said one striking thing which deserves to be remembered. Warning the students against an over-concern for money, or position, or glory, he said: "Some day you will meet a man who cares for none of these things. Then you will know how poor you are."

—Halford E. Luccock

To my children: Nic, Noah, and Nohemi.

A child is the ultimate startup, and I have three.

This makes me rich.

Acknowledgments

In giving advice, seek to help, not please, your friend.
—Solon

M y thanks to all the people who helped me with this book. First, Rick Kot at Viking, because this book was his idea. Furthermore, he tolerated my crazy ideas—including the title and subtitle and having a cover-design contest. Every author should be so lucky to work with an editor like Rick. (The converse is not necessarily true.)

Second, Patty Bozza and Alessandra Lusardi of Viking, and the Portfolio team: Joe Perez, Will Weisser, and Adrian Zackheim, as well as Lisa "Her Highness" Berkowitz. Behind every successful author stands an amazing team.

Third, a group of readers who truly sought to help, not please, me. They spent many hours reading and refining my drafts. My eternal gratitude to: Marylene Delbourg-Delphis, George Grigoryev, Ronit HaNegby, Heidi Mason, Bill Meade, John Michel, Anne P. Mitchell, Lisa Nirell, Bill Reichert, Gary Shaffer, Rick Sklarin, and Andrew Tan.

Fourth, a group of people who contributed by making suggestions, course corrections, and additions. They are: Mohamed Abdel-Rahman, Anupam Anand, Imran Anwar, Dave Baeckelandt, A. J. Balasubramanian, Steve Bengston, David Berg, Scott Butler, Tom Byers, Antonio Carrero, Lilian Chau, Pam Chun, Tom Corr, Stephen Cox, Deborah Vollmer Dahlke, Martin Edic, Bob Elmore, Eric Erickson, Elaine Ferré, Pam Fischer, Sam Hahn, Lenn Hann, Steve Holden, Hilary Horlock, Katherine Hsu, Doug Ito, Bill Joos, John Michel, Cindy Nemeth-Johannes, Tom Kosnik, Pavin Lall, Les Laky, Molly

Lavik, Eric "I'm Open" Lier, Anthony Lloyd, Robert MacGregor, Tom Meade, Chris Melching, Fujio Mimomi, Geoffrey O'Neill, Bola Odulate, Colin Ong, Steve Owlett, Lakiba Pittman, Gina Poss, Julie Pound, Warrick Poyser, the Propon Team, Richard Putz, Anita Rao, Jim Roberts, Marty Rogers, John Roney, Aaron Rosenzweig, Michael Rozenek, Brian Rudolph, David Schlitter, John Scull, Izhar Shay, Marc Sirkin, Marty Stogsdill, Judy Swartley, Russ Taylor, Larry Thompson, Amy Vernetti, Ryan Walcott, Shelly Watson, Tim Wilson, Ryan Wong, and Jan Zones.

Fifth, the people who helped me to market this book: Alyssa Fisher, Sandy Kory, Tess Mayall, Ruey Feng Peh, Shifeng Li, Shyam Sankar, Betty Taylor, and Kai Yang Wang.

Sixth, my loving and lovely wife, Beth. Thank you for bearing with me as I wrote this book during a very busy time in our lives, and for the best twenty years of my life.

Seventh, Sloan Harris of International Creative Management. Thank God for Sloan—otherwise, Rick Kot and Portfolio would have eaten me alive.

Eighth, Patrick Lor and the gang at iStockPhoto.com who helped this graphically challenged author.

Finally, John Baldwin, Ruben Ayala, and Ken Yackel of the Ice Oasis Skating and Hockey Club. Were it not for them, I would have finished this book six months earlier. But then I wouldn't be the best fifty-year-old, transplanted Hawaiian, beginner ice hockey player in Silicon Valley. And this is certainly a desirable niche to fill.

Contents

A friend is one to whom you can pour out the contents of your heart, chaff and grain alike. Knowing that the gentlest of hands will take and sift it, keep what is worth keeping, and with a breath of kindness, blow the rest away.

—anonymous

Read Me First

The most exciting phrase to hear in science, the one that heralds new discoveries, is not "Eureka!" (I found it!) but "That's funny. . . ."
—Isaac Asimov

There are many ways to describe the ebb and flow, yin and yang, bubble-blowing and bubble-bursting phases of business cycles. Here's another one: microscopes and telescopes.

In the microscope phase, there's a cry for level-headed thinking, a return to fundamentals, and going "back to basics." Experts magnify every detail, line item, and expenditure, and then demand full-blown forecasts, protracted market research, and all-encompassing competitive analysis.

In the telescope phase, entrepreneurs bring the future closer. They dream up "the next big thing," change the world, and make late-adopters eat their dust. Lots of money is wasted, but some crazy ideas do stick, and the world moves forward.

When telescopes work, everyone is an astronomer, and the world is full of stars. When they don't, everyone whips out their microscopes, and the world is full of flaws. The reality is that you need both microscopes and telescopes to achieve success.

The problem is that this means gathering information that is spread among hundreds of books, magazines, and conferences. It also means talking to dozens of experts and professionals—if you can get, and afford, an audience. You could spend all your time learning and not doing. And *doing,* not learning to do, is the essence of entrepreneurship.

The Art of the Start alleviates this pain. My goal is to help you use your knowledge, love, and determination to create something great without getting bogged down in theory and unnecessary details. My presumption is that your goal is to change the world—not study it. If your attitude is "Cut the crap and just tell me what I need to do," you've come to the right place.

You might be wondering, Who, exactly, is "you"? The reality is that "entrepreneur" is not a job title. It is the *state of mind* of people who want to alter the future. (It certainly isn't limited to Silicon Valley types seeking venture capital.) Hence, this book is for people in a wide range of startup endeavors:

- guys and gals in garages creating the next great company
- brave souls in established companies bringing new products and services to market
- saints starting schools, churches, and not-for-profits

Great companies. Great divisions. Great schools. Great churches. Great not-for-profits. When it comes to the fundamentals of starting up, they are more alike than they are different. The key to their success is to survive the microscope tasks while bringing the future closer. Let's get started.

Guy Kawasaki
Palo Alto, California
Kawasaki@garage.com

Causation

CHAPTER 1

The Art of Starting

*Everyone should carefully observe which way his heart
draws him, and then choose that way with all his strength.*

—Hasidic saying

GIST (GREAT IDEAS FOR STARTING THINGS)

I use a top-ten list format for all my speeches, and I would love to begin this book with a top-ten list of the most important things an entrepreneur must accomplish. However, there aren't ten—there are only five:

1. **MAKE MEANING** (inspired by John Doerr). The best reason to start an organization is to make meaning—to create a product or service that makes the world a better place. So your first task is to decide how you can make meaning.

2. **MAKE MANTRA.** Forget mission statements; they're long, boring, and irrelevant. No one can ever remember them—much less implement them. Instead, take your meaning and make a mantra out of it. This will set your entire team on the right course.

3. **GET GOING.** Start creating and delivering your product or service. Think soldering irons, compilers, hammers, saws, and AutoCAD—

whatever tools you use to build products and services. Don't focus on pitching, writing, and planning.

4. **DEFINE YOUR BUSINESS MODEL.** No matter what kind of organization you're starting, you have to figure out a way to make money. The greatest idea, technology, product, or service is short-lived without a sustainable business model.

5. **WEAVE A MAT (MILESTONES, ASSUMPTIONS, AND TASKS).** The final step is to compile three lists: (a) major milestones you need to meet; (b) assumptions that are built into your business model; and (c) tasks you need to accomplish to create an organization. This will enforce discipline and keep your organization on track when all hell breaks loose—and all hell will break loose.

MAKE MEANING

I have never thought of writing for reputation and honor. What I have in my heart must come out; that is the reason why I compose.
—Ludwig van Beethoven

Many books about entrepreneurship begin with a rigorous process of self-examination, asking you to determine if you are truly up to the task of starting an organization. Some typical examples are

- Can you work long hours at low wages?
- Can you deal with rejection after rejection?
- Can you handle the responsibility of dozens of employees?

The truth is, it is impossible to answer questions like this in advance, and they ultimately serve no purpose. On the one hand, talk and bravado are cheap. Saying you're willing to do something doesn't mean that you will do it.

On the other hand, realizing that you have doubt and trepidation doesn't mean you won't build a great organization. How you answer these questions now has little predictive power regarding what you'll actually do when you get caught up in a great idea.

The truth is that no one really *knows* if he* is an entrepreneur until he becomes one—and sometimes not even then. There really is only one question you should ask yourself before starting any new venture:

Do I want to make *meaning*?

Meaning is not about money, power, or prestige. It's not even about creating a fun place to work. Among the meanings of "meaning" are to

- Make the world a better place.
- Increase the quality of life.
- Right a terrible wrong.
- Prevent the end of something good.

Goals such as these are a tremendous advantage as you travel down the difficult path ahead. If you answer this question in the negative, you may still be successful, but it will be harder to become so because making meaning is the most powerful motivator there is.

It's taken me twenty years to come to this understanding.

In 1983, when I started in the Macintosh Division of Apple Computer, beating IBM was our reason for existence. We wanted to send IBM back to the typewriter business holding its Selectric typewriter balls.

In 1987, our reason for existence became beating Windows and Microsoft. We wanted to crush Microsoft and force Bill Gates to get a job flipping fish at the Pike Place Market.

In 2004, I am a managing director in an early-stage venture capital firm called Garage Technology Ventures. I want to enable people to create great products, build great companies, and change the world.

The causation of great organizations is the desire to make meaning. Having that desire doesn't guarantee that you'll succeed, but it does mean that if you fail, at least you failed doing something worthwhile.

---

*If only defeating sexism were as simple as throwing in an occasional *he/she, she, her,* or *her*s. I use the masculine pronouns merely as a shortcut. Successful entrepreneurship is blind to gender. Don't look for sexism where none exists.

> **EXERCISE**
>
> Complete this sentence: If your organization never existed, the world would be worse off because _____.

MAKE MANTRA

Close your eyes and think about how you will serve your customers. What kind of meaning do you see your organization making? Most people refer to this as the "Why" or mission statement of an organization.

Crafting a mission statement is usually one of the first steps entrepreneurs undertake. Unfortunately, this process is usually a painful and frustrating experience that results in exceptional mediocrity. This is almost inevitable when a large number of people are commissioned to craft something designed to make an even larger number of people (employees, shareholders, customers, and partners) happy.

The fundamental shortcoming of most mission statements is that everyone expects them to be highfalutin and all-encompassing. The result is a long, boring, commonplace, and pointless joke.* In *The Mission Statement Book,* Jeffrey Abrams provides 301 examples of mission statements that demonstrate that companies are all writing the same mediocre stuff. To wit, this is a partial list of the frequency with which mission statements in Abrams's sample contained the same words:

- Best—94
- Communities—97
- Customers—211

---

*If you insist on creating a mission statement, go to www.artofthestart.com and click on the mission statement generator link (http://www.unitedmedia.com/comics/dilbert/career/bin/ms2.cgi.). This will take you to the Dilbert mission statement generator and save you thousands of dollars.

- Excellence—77
- Leader—106
- Quality—169*

Fortune (or *Forbes,* in my case) favors the bold, so I'll give you some advice that will make life easy for you: Postpone writing your mission statement. You can come up with it later when you're successful and have lots of time and money to waste. (If you're not successful, it won't matter that you didn't develop one.)

Instead of a mission statement and all the baggage that comes with it, craft a mantra for your organization. The definition of *mantra* is

> A sacred verbal formula repeated in prayer, meditation, or incantation, such as an invocation of a god, a magic spell, or a syllable or portion of scripture containing mystical potentialities.[†]

What a great thing a mantra is! How many mission statements evoke such power and emotion?

The beauty of a mantra is that everyone expects it to be short and sweet. (Arguably, the world's shortest mantra is the single Hindi word *Om.*) You may never have to write your mantra down, publish it in your annual report, or print it on posters. Indeed, if you do have to "enforce" your mantra in these ways, it's not the right mantra.

Following are five examples that illustrate the power of a good mantra:

- Authentic athletic performance (Nike).[‡]
- Fun family entertainment (Disney).[ʃ]
- Rewarding everyday moments (Starbucks).[ǁ]
- Think (IBM).
- Winning is everything (Vince Lombardi's Green Bay Packers).

---

*Jeffrey Abrams, *The Mission Statement Book* (Berkeley: Ten Speed Press, 1999), 25–26.
[†]*The American Heritage Dictionary of the English Language,* 4th ed., s.v. *mantra.*
[‡]Scott Bedbury, *A New Brand World: 8 Principles for Achieving Brand Leadership in the 21st Century* (New York: Viking, 2002), 51.
[ʃ]Ibid., 52.
[ǁ]Ibid., 53.

Compare the Starbucks mantra, "Rewarding everyday moments," to the company's mission statement, "Establish Starbucks as the premier purveyor of the finest coffee in the world while maintaining our uncompromising principles while we grow." Which is more memorable?

Imagine that someone asks your parents or your organization's receptionist what you do. Can it get any better than a three-word mantra such as "Authentic athletic performance"?*

EXERCISE

In only the space provided, write your organization's mantra:

_____

A final thought on mantras: Don't confuse mantras and tag lines. A mantra is for your employees; it's a guideline for what they do in their jobs. A tag line is for your customers; it's a guideline for how to use your product or service. For example, Nike's mantra is "Authentic athletic performance." Its tag line is "Just do it."

EXERCISE

The following chart contains the real mission statements of several organizations, and hypothetical mantras that I made up for them. Which do you think is more powerful?

ORGANIZATION	REAL MISSION STATEMENT	HYPOTHETICAL MANTRA
Southwest Airlines	"The mission of Southwest Airlines is dedication to the highest quality of Customer Service delivered with a sense of warmth, friendliness, individual pride, and Company Spirit."	Better than driving.

---

*Actually, it could. Back in the early days, we toyed with "We take the FU out of funding" for Garage's mantra, but we rejected it because it was too long. :-)

ORGANIZATION	REAL MISSION STATEMENT	HYPOTHETICAL MANTRA
Coca-Cola	"The Coca-Cola Company exists to benefit and refresh everyone it touches."	Refresh the world.
Wendy's	"The mission of Wendy's is to deliver superior quality products and services for our customers and communities through leadership innovation and partnerships."	Healthy fast food.
Red Cross	"To help people prevent, prepare for and respond to emergencies."	Stop suffering.
United States Air Force	"To defend the United States and protect its interests through aerospace power."	Kick butt in air and space.
United Way (Hawaii)	"The purpose of Aloha United Way is to provide leadership to bring people together to create a healthier, more compassionate community."	Bring people together.
March of Dimes	"March of Dimes researchers, volunteers, educators, outreach workers and advocates work together to give all babies a fighting chance against the threats to their health: prematurity, birth defects, low birthweight."	Save babies.

GET GOING

The third step is not to fire up Word to write a business plan, launch PowerPoint to craft a pitch, or boot Excel to build a financial projection. Wrong, wrong, wrong!

My goal in giving you this advice is not to reduce the sales of Microsoft Office—remember, I'm off the anti-Microsoft podium. There's a time for using all three applications, but it's not now. What you should do is (a) rein in your anal tendency to craft a document and (b) implement.

This means building a prototype, writing software, launching your Web site, or offering your services. The hardest thing about getting started is getting started. (This is as true for a writer as it is for an entrepreneur.) Remember: No one ever achieved success by *planning* for gold.

You should always be selling—not strategizing about selling. Don't test, test, test—that's a game for big companies. Don't worry about being embarrassed. Don't wait to develop the perfect product or service. Good enough is good enough. There will be plenty of time for refinement later. It's not how great you start—it's how great you end up.

The enemy of activation is cogitation, and at this stage, cogitating the "strategic" issues of research and development is a problem. Questions like, *How far can we leap ahead? What if everyone doesn't like what we do?* and *Should we design for a target customer or make what we would want to use?* are beside the point when you're getting a new venture off the ground.

Instead, observe these key principles of getting going:

- **THINK BIG.** Set your sights high and strive for something grand. If you're going to change the world, you can't do it with milquetoast and boring products or services. Shoot for doing things at least ten times better than the status quo. When Jeff Bezos started Amazon. com, he didn't build a bookstore with a paltry 25,000 more titles than the 250,000-title brick-and-mortar bookstores. He went to 3,000,000 titles in an online bookstore.

- **FIND A FEW SOULMATES.** History loves the notion of the sole innovator: Thomas Edison (light bulb), Steve Jobs (Macintosh), Henry Ford (Model T), Anita Roddick (The Body Shop), Richard Branson (Virgin Airlines). History is wrong. Successful companies are started, and made successful, by at least two, and usually more, soulmates. After the fact, one person may come to be recognized as "the innovator," but it always takes a team of good people to make any venture work.

- **POLARIZE PEOPLE.** When you create a product or service that some people love, don't be surprised when others hate you. Your goal is to catalyze passion—pro or anti. Don't be offended if people take issue with what you've done; the only result that should offend (and scare) you is lack of interest.

Car design is a good example of the love-versus-hate reaction; consider the bifurcation of people's reactions to cars such as the Mini Cooper, Infiniti Fx45, and Toyota Scion xB. People are either devoted fans or relentless critics, and that's good.

Mini Cooper

Photo credit: Photo courtesy MINI USA

Infiniti Fx45

Photo credit: © Nissan (2003). Infiniti and the Infiniti logo are registered trademarks of Nissan North America, Inc.

Toyota Scion xB

Photo credit: Toyota Motor Sales, USA, Inc.

- **DESIGN DIFFERENT.** Depending on what management fad is hot, you might be tempted to believe that there is only one ideal way to design products and services. This isn't true. There is no single best way. Here are four different and valid approaches—and I am sure there are more.

  "I WANT ONE." This is the best kind of market research—the customer and the designer are the same person. Therefore, the customer's voice can reach the designer's mind uncorrupted by corporate politics, reliance on the status quo, and market researchers. Example: Ferdinand Porsche said, "In the beginning I looked around and, not finding the automobile of my dreams, decided to build it myself."*

  "MY EMPLOYER COULDN'T (OR WOULDN'T) DO IT." Not as romantic as "I want one," but this is a credible path. You already understand the customer base, competition, supply sources, and industry contacts because of your background. You still need to build the product or service and get customers, but many questions are already answered. For example, alumni of Unit 8200 of the Israeli Defense Forces went on to create companies such as Checkpoint after developing security software for the military.

  "WHAT THE HELL—IT'S POSSIBLE!" This theory isn't popular when times are tough, and microscopes are flourishing. At these times, the world has turned conservative and demands that every market be "proven." Markets for curve-jumping, paradigm-shifting leaps are seldom proven in advance. For example, when Motorola invented cellular telephones, no one leaped to buy them. At that time, *portable phone* was an oxymoron because phones were always attached to places. There was no market for phones that customers could move.

Forbes FYI (Winter 2003): 21.

"THERE MUST BE A BETTER WAY." The organization born of this philosophy is based on the idealistic notion that you can make the world a better place by doing something new. In many cases, the founders had backgrounds with no logical connection to the business. They simply got an idea and decided to do it. Example: eBay. Pierre Omidyar, the founder, wanted to implement a system for a "perfect market" for the sale of goods. (The story of his girlfriend wanting to sell Pez dispensers was an after-the-fact PR tale.)

- **USE PROTOTYPES AS MARKET RESEARCH.** In the early days of an organization, there is high uncertainty about exactly what you should create and exactly what customers want. In these times, traditional market research is useless—there is no survey or focus group that can predict customer acceptance for a product or service that you may barely be able to describe. Would you buy a new computer with no software, no hard disk, and no color that simulates the real world—including a trash can?*

  The wisest course of action is to take your best shot with a prototype, immediately get it to market, and iterate quickly. If you wait for ideal circumstances in which you have all the information you need (which is impossible), the market will pass you by.

The expected outcome of the "get going" principle is a first release of a product or service. Remember: it won't be perfect. But don't revise your product to get prospective customers to love it. Instead, revise it because customers already love it. Let me put it in religious terms: Some people believe that if they change, God will love them. Others believe that since God loves them, they should change. The latter theory is the prototype to keep in mind for how to get going and keep going for startups.

---

*This isn't how we positioned the first Macintosh, but it's a pretty accurate description of what we had.

DEFINE YOUR BUSINESS MODEL

You want to make meaning. You've come up with a mantra. You've started prototyping your product or service. The fourth step is to define a business model. To do this you need to answer two questions:

- Who has your money in their pockets?
- How are you going to get it into your pocket?

These questions lack subtlety, but they are a useful way to consider the reality of starting an organization—even, and perhaps especially, not-for-profits, which have to fight for money just to stay alive. You can't change the world if you're dead, and when you're out of money you're dead.

More elegantly stated, the first question involves defining your customer and the pain that he feels. The second question centers around creating a sales mechanism to ensure that your revenues exceed your costs. Here are some tips to help you develop your business model:

- **BE SPECIFIC.** The more precisely you can describe your customer, the better. Many entrepreneurs are afraid of being "niched" to death and then not achieving ubiquity. However, most successful companies started off targeting specific markets and grew (often unexpectedly) to great size by addressing other segments. Few started off with grandiose goals and achieved them.

- **KEEP IT SIMPLE.** If you can't describe your business model in ten words or less, you don't have a business model. You should use approximately ten words—and employ them wisely by using simple, everyday terminology. Avoid whatever business jargon is currently hip (*strategic, mission-critical, world-class, synergistic, first-mover, scalable, enterprise-class,* etc.). Business language does not make a business model.* Think of eBay's business model: It charges a listing fee plus a commission. End of story.

---

*Inspired by Michael Shermer, *Why People Believe Weird Things* (New York: A.W.H. Freeman, 2002), 49.

- **COPY SOMEBODY.** Commerce has been around a long time, and by now clever people have pretty much invented every business model that's possible. You can innovate in technology, markets, and customers, but inventing a new business model is a bad bet. Try to relate your business model to one that's already successful and understood. You have plenty of other battles to fight.

My final tip is that you ask women—and only women. My theory is that deep in the DNA of men is a "killer" gene. This gene expresses itself by making men want to kill people, animals, and plants. To a large degree, society has repressed this gene; however, starting an organization whose purpose is to kill another organization is still socially acceptable.

Hence, asking a man about a business model is useless because every business model looks good to someone with the Y chromosome. For example, Sun Microsystems wants to kill Microsoft. When is the last time you bought a computer based on whom the manufacturer wanted to kill?

Women, by contrast, don't have this killer gene. Thus, they are much better judges of the viability of a business model than men are. Don't agree with me? The book *The Darwin Awards* provides irrefutable proof of women's greater common sense. These awards commemorate "those individuals who have removed themselves from the gene pool in a sublimely idiotic fashion."*

For example, in 1998 two construction workers fell to their demise after cutting a circular hole in the floor while they were standing in the middle of the circle.† *The Darwin Awards* contains nine chapters about the stupidity of men, and one chapter about the stupidity of women. I rest my case.

---

*Wendy Northcutt, *The Darwin Awards II* (New York: Dutton, 2001), 2.
†Ibid., 70.

> **EXERCISE**
>
> **Step 1:** Calculate your monthly costs to operate your organization.
>
> **Step 2:** Calculate the gross profit of each unit of your product.
>
> **Step 3:** Divide the results of Step 1 by the results of Step 2.
>
> **Step 4:** Ask a few women if they think you have a chance of selling that many units. If they don't, you don't have a business model.

WEAVE A MAT (MILESTONES, ASSUMPTIONS, AND TASKS)

One definition of *mat* is "a heavy woven net of rope or wire cable placed over a blasting site to keep debris from scattering."[*] Preventing scattering is exactly what you need to do as the fifth, and final, step of launching your enterprise. In this case, MAT stands for milestones, assumptions, and tasks.[†]

The purpose of compiling the MAT is to understand the scope of what you're undertaking, test assumptions quickly, and provide a method to find and fix the large flaws in your thinking.

Milestones

For most people a startup looks as if it must achieve a seemingly unlimited number of goals. However, out of these goals are some that stand head and shoulders above the others. These are the organization's milestones—they mark significant progress along the road to success. There are seven milestones that every startup must focus on. If you miss any of them, your organization might die.

- Prove your concept.
- Complete design specifications.

---

[*]*The American Heritage Dictionary of the English Language,* 4th ed., s.v. *mat.*
[†]Inspired by Rita Gunther McGrath and Ian C. MacMillan, "Discovery-Driven Planning," *Harvard Business Review* (July–August 1995).

- Finish a prototype.
- Raise capital.
- Ship a testable version to customers.
- Ship the final version to customers.
- Achieve breakeven.

These milestones apply to every kind of business. For example, a new school can prove its concept by seeing if two teachers, working as a team, using a new curriculum, can provide more individualized instruction and improve learning in a test classroom. With this proof of concept, the school can then complete the design of its curriculum, raise funds, roll out the prototype, and start teaching classes.

There are other tasks (we'll come to them soon) that are also important to the survival of the organization, but none are as important as these milestones. The timing of these milestones will drive the timing of just about everything else you need to do, so spend 80 percent of your effort on them.

EXERCISE

Take down the corny framed mission statement in your lobby and replace it with a printout of target dates for completion of the seven milestones listed above. Make sure that employees and guests can read it.

Extra Credit

Repeat this procedure for every new product or service. Create a wall of fame to track the history of your organization.

Assumptions

Second, create a comprehensive list of the major assumptions that you are making about the business. These include factors such as

- product or service performance metrics
- market size
- gross margin

- sales calls per salesperson
- conversion rate of prospects to customers
- length of sales cycle
- return on investment for the customer
- technical support calls per unit shipped
- payment cycle for receivables and payables
- compensation requirements
- prices of parts and supplies

Continuously track these assumptions, and when they prove false, react to them quickly. Ideally, you can link these assumptions to one of the seven milestones discussed above. Thus, as you reach a milestone, you can test an assumption.

Tasks

Third, create another comprehensive list—this time of the major tasks that are necessary to design, manufacture, sell, ship, and support your product or service. These are necessary to build an organization, though they are not as critical as the seven milestones. They include

- renting office space
- finding key vendors
- setting up accounting and payroll systems
- filing legal documents
- purchasing insurance policies

The point of the list of tasks is to understand and appreciate the totality of what your organization has to accomplish, and to not let anything slip through the cracks in the early, often euphoric days.

MINICHAPTER: THE ART OF INTERNAL ENTREPRENEURING

Innovation often originates outside existing organizations, in part because successful organizations acquire a commitment to the status quo and a resistance to ideas that might change it.

—Nathan Rosenberg

A large number of aspiring entrepreneurs currently work for big companies. Like all entrepreneurs, they dream of creating innovative products or services and wonder if this can be done internally. The answer is yes. The purpose of this minichapter is to explain how.

The "arts" that this book describes are equally appropriate for internal entrepreneurs—they, too, must innovate, position, pitch, write business plans, bootstrap, recruit, raise capital, partner, establish brands, make rain, and be mensches. But there are special recommendations that apply in this case.

Ironically, many independent entrepreneurs envy the employees of big companies—they think that these lucky souls have humongous financial resources, large sales forces, fully equipped labs, scalable factories, and established brands, plus medical and dental benefits, at their disposal. How wonderful it would be, guys in garages muse, to invent a new product or service with the luxury of such an infrastructure already in place.

Guess again. Creating a new product or service inside such a beast is not necessarily easier; the challenges are just different. I happen to have been part of a "best-case" scenario: the Macintosh Division of Apple. I can explain the success of this internal entrepreneurial effort in two words: *Steve Jobs.* His off-the-scale design talents, maniacal attention to detail, and reality-distorting personality (plus co-founder status) made Macintosh successful. Were it not for Steve Jobs, Macintosh would not exist—or it would have taken the form of an Apple II with a trash can.

But if it takes a Steve Jobs to innovate within large companies, you are undoubtedly thinking, *we might as well give up right now.* While that kind of visionary is in short supply in any business, anyone with guts, vision, and political savvy should be able to set up an entrepreneurial outpost in an established business. I collaborated on this minichapter with Bill Meade, a close friend who helped Hewlett-Packard organize its substantial vault of intellectual property. We came up with this list of recommendations for internal entrepreneurs.

- **PUT THE COMPANY FIRST.** The internal entrepreneur's primary, if not sole, motivation should remain the betterment of the company. Internal entrepreneurship isn't about grabbing attention, building an empire, or setting up a way to catapult out of the company. When you have a good idea for a product or service, it will attract a large number of employees, from the bottom up. They will support you if you're doing it for the company, but not if it's for your personal gain. If you can attract a large number of rank-and-file supporters, you might not be totally dependent on what the "vice presidents" say.

- **KILL THE CASH COWS.** Don't announce this widely, but your charter is often to create the product or service that would put an end to existing products or services. Still, it's better that it's you who's killing your company's cash cows than a competitor or two guys in a garage. Macintosh killed Apple II. Would it have been better for Apple if a competitor had created Macintosh? No way. This recommendation is another reason why it's so important that you've put the company first: What you're doing is bound to be controversial. But if you don't kill the cash cows, someone external will.

- **STAY UNDER THE RADAR.** Two guys in a garage should try to get as much attention as they can. Awareness of their efforts makes it easier to raise money, establish partnerships, close sales, and recruit employees. However, the opposite holds true for internal entrepreneurs. You want to be left alone until either your project is too far along to ignore or the rest of the company realizes that it's needed. The higher you go in a company, the fewer people are going to understand what you're trying to do. This is because the higher you go, the more people want to maintain the status quo and protect their positions.

- **FIND A GODFATHER.** In many companies, there are godfather figures. These are people who have paid their dues and are safe from everyday petty politics. They are relatively untouchable and usually have the attention and respect of top management. Internal entrepreneurs should find a godfather to support their projects by providing advice, technical and marketing insights, and protection—if it comes to the point where you need protection.

- **GET A SEPARATE BUILDING.** An internal entrepreneur, sitting in the main flow of a big company, will die by a thousand cuts as each department manager explains why this new project is a bad idea. "The new always looks so puny—so unpromising—next to the reality of the massive, ongoing business."* The Macintosh Division started in a building that was far enough away from the rest of Apple that it stayed out of the daily grind, but was close enough to obtain corporate resources. A separate building will keep your efforts under the radar and foster ésprit de corps among your merry band of pirates. The ideal distance from the corporate pukes is between one-quarter mile and two miles—that is, close enough to get to, but far enough to discourage overly frequent visits.

- **GIVE HOPE TO THE HOPEFUL.** Inside every corporate cynic who thinks that "this company is too big to innovate" is an idealist who would like to see it happen. Good people in big companies are tired of being ignored, forgotten, humiliated, and forced into submission. They may be trampled, but they are not dead. When you show them that you're driving a stake in the heart of the status quo, you will attract support and resources. Then your goal is to advance these people from wanting to see innovation happen to helping you make it happen.

- **ANTICIPATE, THEN JUMP ON, TECTONIC SHIFTS.** Structural deformations in a company are a good thing for internal entrepreneurs. Whether caused by external factors such as changes in the marketplace or internal factors such as a new CEO, tectonic shifts signal changes and may create an opportunity for your efforts. Effective internal entrepreneurs anticipate these shifts and are ready to unveil new products or services when they occur: "Look what we've been working on." By contrast, corporate pukes say, "Now I

---

*Peter F. Drucker, *Innovation and Entrepreneurship: Practice and Principles* (New York: Harper & Row, 1985), 162.

see the shift. If you give me permission, six months, and a team of analysts, I can come up with a new product strategy."

- **BUILD ON WHAT EXISTS.** The downside of trying to innovate within a big company is clear and well documented, but there are also benefits to doing so. Don't hesitate to utilize the existing infrastructure to make innovation easier—start by stealing, if you have to. You'll not only garner resources, but also make friends as other employees begin to feel as if they are part of your team. If you try to roll your own solutions (as an extreme example, building your own factory), you'll only make enemies. The last thing a startup inside a big company needs is internal enemies—there will be enough enemies in the marketplace.

- **COLLECT AND SHARE DATA.** The day will inevitably arrive when a bean counter or lawyer is suddenly going to take notice of you and question the reasons for your project's existence. If you're lucky, this will happen later rather than sooner, but it will happen. Prepare for that day by (1) collecting data about how much you've spent and how much you've accomplished and (2) then sharing it openly. In big companies, data suppresses antibodies, but it might be too late to get the data once the antibodies appear.

- **LET THE VICE PRESIDENTS COME TO YOU.** Quick question: Do you think that your first step should be to get your vice president to sign off on your project? It shouldn't be. This is one of the last steps. A vice president will "own" your idea and support it more if he "discovers" it and then approaches you about sponsoring it. You may have to ensure that a vice president "accidentally" makes that discovery when the time is right, but this is not the same as seeking permission to get started.

- **DISMANTLE WHEN DONE.** The beauty of an internal entrepreneurial group is that it can rapidly develop new products and services. Unfortunately, the very cohesiveness that makes it so effective can lead to its downfall later if it remains separate (and usually aloof) from the rest of the organization. Its effectiveness declines further as its members come to believe that only they "know" what to do, and the entrepreneurial group creates its own, new bureaucracy.* If the product or service is successful, consider dismantling the group and integrating it into the larger organization. Then create a new group to jump ahead again.

- **REBOOT YOUR BRAIN.** Many internal entrepreneurs will find that the rest of this book prescribes actions that are contrary to what they've experienced, learned, and maybe even taught in big companies. The reality is that starting something within an existing company requires adopting new patterns of behavior—essentially, rebooting your brain. The following table will prepare you for what's to come:

TOPIC	BIG COMPANY	STARTUP
Positioning	Being all things to all people	Finding a niche and dominating it
Pitching	Sixty slides, 120 minutes, and fourteen-point font	Ten slides, twenty minutes, and thirty-point font
Writing a Business Plan	Two hundred pages of extrapolation from historical data	Twenty pages of wishful thinking
Bootstrapping	Staying in a Hyatt Regency instead of a Ritz Carlton	Staying with a college buddy instead of a Motel Six
Recruiting	Corporate headhunters screening candidates with *Fortune* 500 or Big Four track records	Sucking in people who "get it" and are willing to risk their careers for stock options
Partnering	Negotiating I-win/you-lose deals that the press will like	Piggybacking on others to increase sales
Branding	Advertising during the Super Bowl	Evangelizing in the trenches
Rainmaking	Spiffs for resellers and commissions for sales reps	Sucking up, down, and across
Being a Mensch	Calling the legal department	Helping people who can't help you

*Andrew Hargadon, *How Breakthroughs Happen: The Surprising Truth About How Companies Innovate* (Boston: Harvard Business School Press, 2003), 116–17.

FAQ (FREQUENTLY AVOIDED QUESTIONS)

Q. I admit it: I'm scared. I can't afford to quit my current job. Is this a sign that
I don't have what it takes to succeed? Am I not truly committed?

A. You should be scared. If you aren't scared, something is wrong with
you. Your fears are not a sign that you don't have the right stuff. In the
beginning, every entrepreneur is scared. It's just that some deceive
themselves about it, and others don't.

You can reduce these fears by diving into the business and making
a little progress every day. One day you'll wake up and you won't be
afraid anymore—or at least you'll have a whole new set of fears.

No matter what, never admit that you're scared to other employees.
A CEO can never have a bad day. But don't go overboard, either, and
act as if you have no concerns, because then they will know you're
scared stiff.

Q. Should I share my secret ideas with anybody other than my dog?

A. The only thing worse than a paranoid entrepreneur is a paranoid entrepreneur who talks to his dog. There is much more to gain—feedback, connections, opened doors—by freely discussing your idea than
there is to lose. If simply discussing your idea makes it indefensible,
you don't have much of an idea in the first place. (See the FAQ section
of Chapter 7, "The Art of Raising Capital," for a detailed discussion
of nondisclosure agreements.)

Q. How far along should I be before I start talking to people about what I'm
doing?

A. Start right away. By doing so you'll be constantly mulling over your
idea—as both a foreground and background task. The more people
you talk to, the richer your thoughts will be. If it's just you staring at
your navel, all you'll see is lint building up.

Q. How do you know if it's time to give up rather than continuing to pursue a
doomed venture?

A. The old platitude is that good entrepreneurs never give up. This is fine
for books and speeches, but not for the real world. If three close
friends tell you to give up, you should listen. As the saying goes, when
three people tell you you're drunk, you should take a cab home. It's
okay to fail as long as you try again.

Q. I think that I have a great idea, but I don't have a business background. What should I do now?

A. First, if all you've done is come up with a great idea—for example, "a new computer operating system that's fast, elegant, and bug free"— but you can't implement it, then you have nothing. In this case, don't waste anyone's time until you've found other people who can do the engineering.

Assuming that you can implement, there are two kinds of people you can recruit. First, you can get a mentor. This would be an older person who is willing to coach you from time to time but never actually do any work. Second, you could get a business partner. This is someone who's willing to work side by side with you—even on a part-time basis—whose skill set complements yours. Either kind of person can make a big difference in your business.

Q. When should I worry about looking like a real business, with business cards, letterhead, and an office?

A. Make business cards and letterhead immediately. Spend a few bucks and get them designed by a professional or don't do them at all. Ensure that the smallest type size is twelve points. An office isn't necessary until customers are coming to see you, or you run out of space for the team.

Q. Do I need a Web site?

A. Yes, particularly if you're going to raise money, serve lots of customers, change the world in a big way, and achieve liquidity. Customers, partners, and investors will look for your Web site from the very start.

RECOMMENDED READING

Christensen, Clayton. *The Innovator's Dilemma: When New Technologies Cause Great Firms to Fail.* New York: HarperBusiness, 1997.

Drucker, Peter F. *Innovation and Entrepreneurship: Practice and Principles.* New York: Harper & Row, 1985.

Hargadon, Andrew. *How Breakthroughs Happen: The Surprising Truth About How Companies Innovate.* Boston: Harvard Business School Press, 2003.

Kuhn, Thomas. *The Structure of Scientific Revolutions.* Chicago: University of Chicago Press, 1962.

Shekerjian, Denise. *Uncommon Genius: How Great Ideas Are Born.* New York: Penguin Books, 1990.

Ueland, Brenda. *If You Want to Write.* St. Paul: Graywolf Press, 1987.

Utterback, James M. *Mastering the Dynamics of Innovation: How Companies Can Seize Opportunities in the Face of Technological Change.* Boston: Harvard Business School Press, 1994.

Articulation

CHAPTER 2

The Art of Positioning

Allow me to introduce myself. My name is Wile E. Coyote . . . Genius. I am not selling anything, nor am I working my way through college, so let's get down to cases. You are a rabbit, and I am going to eat you for supper. Now, don't try to get away! I am more muscular, more cunning, faster, and larger than you are . . . and I'm a genius. Why, you could hardly pass the entrance examinations to kindergarten. So, I'll give you the customary two minutes to say your prayers.
—The Bugs Bunny/Road Runner Movie (1979)

GIST

Most people consider "positioning" an unnatural act foisted upon them by marketing dweebs who are assisted by highly paid and clueless consultants. In truth, positioning goes far beyond a management offsite or exercise. When done properly, it represents the heart and soul of a new organization, stating clearly

- why the founders started the organization
- why customers should patronize it
- why good people should work at it

Wile E. Coyote understands positioning better than most entrepreneurs: He's a coyote, and he's going to eat the rabbit for lunch. Organizations should position themselves with comparable clarity by explaining exactly what it is they do. The art of positioning really comes down to nothing more than answering that one simple question:

What do you do?

Developing a good answer to this question involves seizing the high ground for your organization and establishing precisely how it differs from the mass of competition. Then you must communicate this message to the marketplace. You will learn how to do both in a short, differentiated, and powerful way in this chapter.

SEIZE THE HIGH GROUND

Unless you are a rabbit about to be devoured by a coyote, good positioning is inspiring and energizing. It does not allow itself to get mucked up in money, market share, and management egos. These are the qualities to aspire to:

- **POSITIVE.** Entrepreneurship isn't war, so you don't describe your enterprise in warlike terms. Your organization's purpose is not to put another organization out of business. Customers don't care if you want to destroy the competition. They want to know what benefits they derive from patronizing your company or service.

- **CUSTOMER-CENTRIC.** Positioning is about what you do for your customers—not about what *you* want to become. Announcing that your organization is "the leading company" is egocentric, not customer-centric. It's also impractical: How can you prove you're the leader? How can you prevent another organization from declaring that *it* is the leader—just as you have?

- **EMPOWERING.** Employees must believe that what you do (that is, your positioning) makes the world a better place. The employees of eBay, for example, believe they enable people to gain financial success. This attitude empowers the employees to exceed their limits—and to enjoy doing so.

The Toyota Prius is a good example of high-ground positioning. The car gets fifty-five miles per gallon of gas by using a hybrid of an electric motor and a gasoline engine. It's not fast, sexy, or luxurious. But it's inexpensive to buy and inexpensive to operate, qualities that position it powerfully and uniquely.

In addition to seizing the high ground, good positioning is a workhorse. It is practical and serves tactical and strategic purposes that are easily understood and believed by customers, vendors, employees, journalists, and partners. Thus, good positioning also embodies these qualities:

- **SELF-EXPLANATORY.** Good positioning states its case unequivocally. It embodies such qualities as saving money and increasing revenue, as well as loftier concepts such as peace of mind, enlightenment, and joy.

- **SPECIFIC.** Good positioning targets the intended customer. If you are the target customer, you immediately understand that. If you're not, you understand that, too. For example, "increase the security of Web sites" is a mediocre and vague value proposition, compared to "reduce the risk of fraud for commercial banks in their online transactions."

- **CORE.** The core competencies of your organization—not ancillary products or services—are the basis of good positioning. For example, Apple Computer's positioning focuses on its ability to create innovative devices. It cannot tell a good story about information technology consulting services.

- **RELEVANT.** The flip side of an organization's core competencies is the core needs of customers. If your core competencies and their core needs aren't well matched, your organization and your positioning will not be attractive to them.

- **LONG-LASTING.** Bad positioning for IBM in its early years would have been "Provide cash registers to stores." Even worse was the decision to name a company National Cash Register.* Aim for positioning that will last one hundred years.

- **DIFFERENTIATED.** Your positioning should not sound like your competitor's. Unfortunately, many companies craft positioning as if there *is* no competition—or as if the only competition is totally incompetent. This is seldom the case. (More about this in the section "Apply the Opposite Test" later in this chapter.)

EXERCISE

Review your positioning. Pick your reaction:
a) Pride because you've achieved laserlike focus on what you stand for.
b) Relief because you've mentioned every possible constituency and customer.

NICHE THYSELF

When F. W. Woolworth opened his first store, a merchant on the same street tried to fight the new competition. He hung out a big sign: "Doing business in this same spot for over fifty years." The next day Woolworth also put out a sign. It read: "Established a week ago: no old stock."

—Peter Hay, *The Book of Business Anecdotes*

Many entrepreneurs try to avoid market niches. They are afraid of getting locked out of important sectors, submaximizing sales, and putting all their eggs in one basket. They strive for broad appeal to large, horizontal markets because they see successful companies that are broad-based and assume that they must be, too.

---

*IBM is the acronym for International Business Machines. While IBM sells more than "business machines," it didn't cubbyhole itself into the cash register market.

Take Microsoft, for example. Who wouldn't want to be Microsoft? Circa 2004, having defeated the Department of Justice, it sells operating systems for personal computers, servers, PDAs, and phones, as well as application software for Windows and Macintosh, plus online access, games for personal computers, and its own line of gaming hardware.

You might think that to build the next Microsoft, you'd have to launch a multiprong attack. Nothing could be further from the right approach. To build the next Microsoft, you have to start in a small niche, establish a beachhead,* and (with luck) move out from there.

Furthermore, you might think that Microsoft started out broad, which is how they now dominate the computer business. To set the record straight, Microsoft started in a sliver of a sector: a programming language called BASIC for an operating system called CPM.

As a startup, you're trying to start a fire with matches, not flamethrowers. (Hence, the design of this book's cover.) Few startup

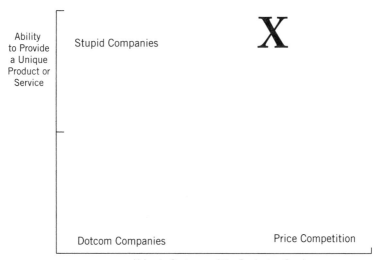

*A *beachhead*, in this context, means a market that is small enough so that larger competitors are not already going after it, and big enough so that if you're successful, you can reach critical mass and profitability with it.

organizations can afford or manage a flamethrower. In other words, put one niche in your basket, hatch it, put another niche in your basket, hatch it . . . and soon you'll have a whole bunch of niches that add up to market domination.

The diagram on the previous page provides a conceptual framework for niche marketing. The vertical axis represents your organization's ability to provide a unique product or service. The higher you are, the more you are able to provide something that is different from everything else in the marketplace. The horizontal axis represents how important your good or service is to the customer. The further to the right you are, the more valuable the good or service. Let's analyze the four corners of this chart:

- **UPPER LEFT.** This is the position that stupid companies occupy. They are producing products or services that no one cares about, but are unique.

- **UPPER RIGHT.** This is the corner you want to occupy. It's where customers most appreciate you and margins are good because you provide something unique that they strongly desire.

- **LOWER LEFT.** Looking back, this is the corner that many dotcom companies occupied. They were providing goods and services nobody cared about, and many companies were doing the same. Other than that, everything was great.

- **LOWER RIGHT.** The problem with this corner is that life is a continuous price war. Sure, people want to buy what you make, but lots of other companies have similar offerings. You can be successful here, but life is a grind.

Accurately assessing the location of your organization on this chart is a difficult task. Most organizations turn it into an exercise in wishful thinking: What parameters can we use that put us in the upper right position? You'd be amazed at what labels companies use to accomplish this goal, but the only relevant parameters are value to the customer and unique ability to provide.

DON'T COMPROMISE ON YOUR NAME

A remarkable name for your organization, product, or service is like pornography: It's hard to define, but you know it when you see it. Coming up with a good name is easier than creating a product or service, but you wouldn't think so based on the atrocities out there.

Spend the time and effort to come up with a good name—it makes positioning easier. Here are some tips for the process:

- **HAVE A FIRST INITIAL THAT'S EARLY IN THE ALPHABET.** Someday your organization's, product's, or service's name will appear in an alphabetical list. Better to be early in the list than later. Imagine, for example, a trade show with a thousand exhibitors. Do you want to be in the first third or last third of the show's directory?

  Also, avoid words that begin with X or Z because they are difficult to spell out after hearing them. For example, if you heard "Xylinx," would you think that it's spelled "Xylinx" or "Zylinx"?

- **AVOID NUMBERS.** They are bad ideas for names because people won't remember whether to use numerals (123) or to spell out the number (One Two Three).

- **PICK A NAME WITH "VERB POTENTIAL."** In a perfect world, your name enters the mainstream vernacular and becomes a verb. For example, people "xerox" documents—as opposed to photocopy them.

  More recently, people "google" words instead of "searching for them on the Internet." Names that work as verbs are short (no more than two or three syllables) and not tongue twisters.

EXERCISE

See if the name you're considering works in this sentence: "_____ it."

AWOA (a word on acronyms): Avoid multiple-word names unless the first word has solid verb potential (for example, "Google Technology Corporation" would still be fine) or the acronym spells out something clever. For example, the name Hawaiian Islands Ministry, a parachurch organization that trains pastors and ministers, becomes "HIM"—a clever homonym with "hymn" and a play on "Him," that is, God.

- **SOUND DIFFERENT (AS OPPOSED TO "THINK DIFFERENT").** The name should sound like nothing else. For (a bad) example: Claris, Clarins, Claritin, and Claria. It's hard to remember which name refers to software, cosmetics, antihistamines, or online marketing. Even if you did remember, it's likely that you would associate all four words with one category, and that can't be good in three of four instances.

- **SOUND LOGICAL.** In addition to sounding different, your names should also sound logical. That is, they should "match" what you do. A good example of this is the names of the Pokémon characters. They are among the most clever examples of naming that you'll come across. Take Geodude and Lickitung, for example.

  Ask your kids to show you the cards of the characters Beautifly, Delcatty, Flygon, and Huntail, and you'll see what I mean about logical names and good positioning.

- **AVOID THE TRENDY.** With hindsight, we made two mistakes naming Garage Technology Ventures when we started it in 1997. First, we initially called the company "garage.com." Unfortunately, *dotcom* acquired negative connotations when the Internet tide went out because it came to stand for companies run by people without business acumen in markets without business models.

  The second mistake was lowercasing the "g" in *garage.com*. It was a silly act of pseudohumility, but those were silly times. The problem with the lowercase "g" was that it was hard to pick it out in blocks of text. The visual cue that the word was a proper noun wasn't there—you'd think that someone named guy (sic) would know this. Also, no one could really figure out what to do when a sentence started with "garage.com"—should it be capitalized or not?

The bottom line, in hindsight, is that you should come up with a name that will endure for decades, and save your cleverness for the features of your products and services.

On the other hand, consider the name Krispy Kreme. It doesn't start with a letter early in the alphabet, and both "crispy" and "cream" are spelled incorrectly. Furthermore, the company's donuts are neither crispy nor creamy. What this proves is that if you have a truly great product, it can overcome anything.

One last example: I saw a great name for a company in a restroom at the Calgary International Airport. The company sells billboard advertising space in restrooms, and its name was Flushmedia. Brilliant.

MAKE IT PERSONAL

To his dog, every man is Napoleon; hence the constant popularity of dogs.

—Aldous Huxley

I recently met an entrepreneur who wanted to start an online service to enable people to create trusts for their pets. She was concerned that sometimes people died before their animals. Her pitch hinged on the fact that nine million pets are euthanized every year in the United States.

My first reaction, as a venture capitalist, was that nine million pets may get euthanized, but not all of them because their owners died. Few are probably euthanized for this reason, so the market isn't as big as she thinks. My second reaction, as a dog owner (Rocky Kawasaki, boxer), was that she was right: What will happen to Rocky? He wasn't included in any of my family's wills and trusts.

The lesson is this: Position your product or service in the most personal way that you can. "What happens to Rocky?" is much more powerful than "What happens to the nine million pets?" If you hook me with a personal concern about my own dog, I can extrapolate

IMPERSONAL	PERSONAL
Our operating system is an industry standard that enables MIS departments to maintain control and reduce costs.	Our operating system enables you to be more creative and productive.
Reduce the size of the global ozone hole.	Prevent you from getting melanoma.
Dozens of airplanes flying in a hub-and-spoke pattern around the United States.	"You are now free to move about the country."
Increasing the mean test scores for children in your school district.	Ensuring that Johnny can read.

this to the millions of other people who are concerned about their pets.

Positioning is more powerful when it's personal because potential customers don't have to take the step of imagining how a product or service fills a need.

SPEAK "ENGLISH"

Ask yourself, did it . . . catch my attention? Hold my interest? Pierce my armor? Talk English? Center on "me"? Make a point?
—Allen Kay, advertising maven, on what makes a good ad

A company CEO showed up one day at Garage and pitched us with the following positioning statement: "Utilizing the 2048-bit Diffie-Hellman key exchange and 168-bit triple-DES, we provide intrusion protection for digital voice, fax, and wireless communications."

To encryption experts, this statement would mean a lot. For the rest of us, the CEO might as well have been speaking in Greek. With our help, he changed his positioning statement to "We safeguard your communications."

If the client had let me, I would have further reduced it to a mantra of "secure communications."

No matter what you're selling or who you're selling it to, use plain words to describe what you do. Whatever jargon is the *lingua franca* of your industry, remember that a lot more people than insiders need to understand what you do.

EXERCISE

Delete all the acronyms and technical terms from your positioning statement. Is it any weaker?

APPLY THE OPPOSITE TEST

Most companies use the same terms to describe their product or service. It's as if they all believe that their prospective customers have been living on a desert island and have never before heard a product or service referred to as "high-quality," "robust," "easy-to-use," "fast," or "safe."

To see what I mean, apply the Opposite Test: Do you describe your offering in a way that is opposite to that of your competition? If you do, then you're saying something different. If you don't, then your descriptions are impotent.

For example, it would be fine to describe your product as "intuitive, secure, fast, and scalable" if your competition describes its product as "hard-to-use, vulnerable, slow, and limited." However, this probably isn't the case, so you're saying nothing.

ADJECTIVE	PROOF POINT
Intuitive	You can set it up in one day, and end users need no training.
Secure	No one has ever hacked it.
Fast	Real-world results show a fivefold improvement in throughput.
Scalable	It has handled as many as 20,000 transactions per second.

A far better way to distinguish your product is to offer concrete proof points so that people can deduce its unique qualities.

Obviously, there are occasions when you do not have the luxury of using this many words to make your point. But this sort of restriction is seldom justification to resort to commonplace and meaningless adjectives. Find unique language or offer scientific proof points, and don't be tempted to think that you have the only product described with such overfamiliar adjectives as *intuitive, secure, fast,* and *scalable.*

CASCADE THE MESSAGE

Crafting the positioning of an organization is a demanding process, but well worth the effort. It's a pity that many companies get to this point and then do nothing more than send out a halfhearted internal memo or stick a rote positioning statement in an annual report. For shame.

A critical step in any positioning process is to ensure that people from the marketing department and top of the organization right down to temps and consultants understand the positioning. You can achieve this by providing a short document detailing your proposal and discussing it in all-hands meetings. Managers should ensure that all employees know it. Think of a waterfall cascading down a mountain— not just the summit is wet.

EXERCISE

Ask your receptionist what your organization does.

Extra Credit

Ask your latest hires why they joined the organization. Their answers provide a rich vein for a good and true positioning statement because they have a fresh, outward-facing perspective.

And don't forget your directors and advisors. You'd be amazed at how many board members cannot effectively describe what an organization does. You'd think that because they "run" the place, they'd know its mandate exactly. In actuality, they're usually far removed from what's really going on—much less what should be going on.

The bottom line is that communicating the positioning of an organization is not just marketing's and management's job: It's every employee's job. This is so important that you need to repeat the process as employees come and go—and even the ones who remain need refreshers on the positioning. A six-month interval is about right.

FLOW WITH THE GO

While you cannot let the market position you, it's also true that you cannot ultimately "control" your positioning.

You do the best you can to craft a good message and cascade it to your employees, customers, and partners. But then the market does a strange, powerful, sometimes frustrating, but often wonderful thing: It decides on its own. This can happen because unintended customers are using your product or service in unintended ways. For example, a spreadsheet/database/word-processing computer becomes a desktop publisher's tool.

When this happens, (a) don't freak out, and (b) listen to what the market is telling you. Perhaps it has done you a favor and found a natural positioning for you. Is it one you can live with? In the end, it's better to flow with what's going than to try to prop up the unnatural positioning you've concocted.

EXERCISE

Step 1: Write a one-paragraph description of your customer's experience when he's using your product or service.

Step 2: Call up a customer and have him write a one-paragraph description of using your product or service.

Step 3: Compare the two descriptions.

FAQ

Q. Should I use a PR firm to craft a positioning statement for my organization?

A. You should never hand the task of positioning over to a PR firm (or any other external organization). It is way too important a job to delegate. Positioning is a fundamental task, so don't wimp out on it.

Q. Is there a strategic advantage in appearing to be "the little guy"? Or, should I try to project a larger, more established image?

A. Lying doesn't scale. Once you start deceiving people, you have to keep track of how you deceived them. This will get more complex, the more people you meet. You should always project what you are. This is not to say that you go out of your way to look undercapitalized, premature, and weak, if that, in fact, is what you are, but don't try to act like General Motors if you're not General Motors.

Q. Should we take into account the availability of domain names when we name the organization?

A. Yes, absolutely. It's not just cool to have a domain name, it's essential that you have one that customers, partners, and investors can easily remember and use.

Q. Do I need to think ahead and consider exit strategies when I think about positioning?

A. I don't know how an exit strategy (which you have no control over) would change your positioning. Build a great organization—one aspect of which will be good positioning. Don't worry about exit strategies—and certainly don't worry about how exit strategies should or could affect your positioning.

RECOMMENDED READING

Trout, Jack. *The New Positioning: The Latest on the World's #1 Business Strategy.* New York: McGraw-Hill, 1995.

CHAPTER 3

The Art of Pitching

Mend your speech a little, lest it may mar your fortunes.

—Shakespeare, *King Lear*

GIST

Forget "I think, therefore I am." For entrepreneurs, the salient phrase is "I pitch, therefore I am." Pitching isn't only useful for raising money—it's an essential tool for reaching agreement on any subject. Agreement can yield many outcomes: management buy-in for developing a product or service, closing a sale, securing a partnership, recruiting an employee, or securing an investment.

Question: How can you tell if an entrepreneur is pitching?

Answer: His lips are moving.

I've long been an evangelist for better pitching because I suffer from a medical condition called tinnitus. This involves a constant ringing in my right ear. I've been to many specialists, and the bottom line is that no one knows what causes it—much less how to cure it.

I've been told to reduce my intake of salt (fat chance for a Japanese-American who loves miso soup and sushi); consume less chocolate, wine, and cheese (fat chance for an American-Japanese living in California); and worry less and sleep more (fat chance for a CEO of a tech company in Silicon Valley). I have another explanation for my medical mystery: The ringing is caused by listening to thousands of lousy pitches.

The gist of pitching is to get off to a fast start, explain the relevance of what you do, stay at a high level, listen to audience reaction, and then pitch over and over again until you get it right. In this chapter, you'll learn how to pitch your organization and product or service in a shorter, simpler, and more effective way.

EXPLAIN YOURSELF IN THE FIRST MINUTE

I've never sat through a pitch by an entrepreneur trying to raise money, an employee trying to get management approval for a new product, or a not-for-profit hoping to secure a grant and thought, *I wish the speaker had spent the first fifteen minutes explaining his life story.* While you're busy warming them up, your listeners are inevitably wondering, *What does his organization* do?

This information is the anchor, foundation, or beachhead—whatever metaphor you want to use—that your audience needs for the pitch to go well. Do everyone a favor: Answer that question in the first minute. Once the audience has learned what you do, they can listen to everything else with a more focused perspective and cut you the slack to indulge in a few digressions.

EXERCISE

Set a timer to one minute. Give your current pitch until the timer goes off. Ask the audience to write down one sentence that explains what your organization does. Collect the answers and compare them to what you think you said.

Unfortunately, many entrepreneurs still believe that a pitch is a narrative whose opening chapter must always be autobiographical. From this heartfelt tale, the audience is supposed to divine what business the organization is in and what the product does.

Think again. It works in the opposite way: First establish what you do, and then the audience can comprehend, or at least deduce, the particulars of your business. Clear the air at the start of your pitch, and don't let anyone have to guess what you do. Make it short and sweet:

- We sell software.
- We sell hardware.
- We teach underprivileged kids.
- We help sinners.
- We prevent child abuse.

ANSWER THE LITTLE MAN

Bill Joos, my colleague at Garage, told me that when he started his career at IBM, the company trained him to imagine there was a little man sitting on his shoulder during presentations. Every time Bill said something, the little man would whisper, "So what?" to him.

Every entrepreneur should carry this little man on his shoulder and listen to him. Unfortunately, most people are either missing the little man, or, like me, they have tinnitus. Remember: The significance of what you're saying is not always self-evident, let alone shocking and awe-inspiring.

Every time you make a statement, imagine the little man's asking his question. After you answer it, follow with the two most powerful words in a pitch: "For instance, . . ."* and then discuss a real-world use or scenario of a feature of your product or service.

Nothing in a pitch is more powerful than combining an answer to "So what?" with "For instance, . . ."

*Richard C. Borden, *Public Speaking—as Listeners Like It!* (New York: Harper & Brothers, 1935), 53.

YOU SAID	LITTLE MAN ASKED	YOU REPLIED	THEN YOU ELABORATED
"We use digital signal processing in our hearing aids."	"So what?"	"Our product increases the clarity of sounds."	"For instance, if you're at a cocktail party with many conversations going on around you, you'll be able to hear what people are saying to you."
"We provide 128-bit encryption in a portable device."	"So what?"	"It's harder than hell to break into our system."	"For instance, if you're in a hotel room and want to have a secure telephone conversation with your headquarters."
"Ms. (big name Celebrity) is on our advisory board."	"So what?"	"What we're doing is interesting enough to attract top talent."	"For instance, she has already opened doors for us in her industry."
"We use Montessori methods in our new school."	"So what?"	"Our school focuses on children as individuals and enables them to learn to manage their own study independently."	"For instance, we enable children who are gifted in specific areas to proceed in advance of the rest of the students."

KNOW YOUR AUDIENCE

Novice entrepreneurs believe that the foundation of a great pitch is the ability to spontaneously generate bull secretion (BS). They're wrong. The foundation of a great pitch is the research that you do before the meeting starts.

First, learn what's important to your audience. You can get this information from your "sponsor" for the meeting by asking the following questions in advance:

- What are the three most important things you would like to learn about our organization?

- What attracted you to our idea and convinced you to give us an opportunity to meet?

- Are there any special issues, questions, or landmines I should be prepared for in the meeting?

- How old will the oldest person in the meeting be? (You'll soon see why you need to know this.)

Second, visit the organization's Web site, use Google searches, read reports, and talk to your industry contacts to gather core information about the audience. These are the areas to investigate:

- **ORGANIZATION BACKGROUND.** What is the organization's mission statement? What was the organization's genesis? Who funded it? Who founded it?

- **EXECUTIVES.** Who works there? What organizations did they work for in their previous positions? Where did they go to school? What boards and other organizations do they work with now?

- **CURRENT EFFORTS.** Questions in this area will vary according to the type of organization you're starting and what you're trying to obtain. Generally, you need to determine exactly what the organization is doing and what its directions are.

Third, brainstorm with your team to find connections, hooks, and angles to make the pitch powerful and meaningful. The possibilities are many, but figuring them out while you're in front of the audience is difficult to do. The key is to conduct this research in advance when you're under little pressure.

OBSERVE THE 10/20/30 RULE

I've never heard a pitch that was too short. A pitch can't be too short because a good one will motivate listeners to ask questions that extend it. Here is a good guideline for the content, length, and font of a good pitch:

- ten slides
- twenty minutes
- thirty-point–font text

Ten Slides

You should be so lucky that your audience remembers one thing about your pitch: what your organization does. Right there, your pitch would be better than 90 percent of the competition's. Remember: You want to communicate "enough," not everything.

"Enough" means enough to get you to the next step—whatever that next step may be. For funding, the next step is meeting with more partners in the firm. For a sale, the next step is a test installation or small purchase. For partnering, the next step is meeting with more people within the organization.

Understand this: The purpose of a pitch is to stimulate interest, not to close a deal. Thus, the recommended number of slides for a pitch is small—ten or so. This seemingly impossibly low number forces you to concentrate on the absolute essentials. You can add a few more, but you should never exceed twenty slides. The fewer slides you need, the more compelling your idea.

Following are three tables that explain the essential slides for three kinds of pitches:

- investor pitch for profit and not-for-profit organizations
- sales pitch to use on a prospective customer
- partner pitch to use on potential partner

A word about liquidity: Although no entrepreneur knows when, how, or if he will achieve liquidity, many insist on including a slide that says, "There are two liquidity options: an IPO or an acquisition." Duh, that's really informative. If an investor asks about your exit strategy, it usually indicates he's clueless. If you answer with these two options, it shows that you have a lot in common with him.

The only time you should include a slide about liquidity is when you can list at least five potential acquirers that the investor is unlikely to know about—this shows that you truly know the industry. By contrast, saying that Microsoft, or the Microsoft of your industry, will buy you will scare off all but the dumbest investors.

Behind your ten slides, you can keep a few that go into greater detail about your technology, marketing, current customers, and other key strategies. If you're asked for a more in-depth explanation, it's nice to have these done in advance. However, they usually don't belong in the set of ten most important slides.

Twenty Minutes

Most appointments are made for an hour; however, you should be able to give your pitch in twenty minutes. There are two reasons for this. First, you may not get one hour if the previous meeting is running late.

Second, you want ample time for discussion. Whether it's twenty minutes of presentation and then forty minutes of discussion or a sequence of slide/discussion, slide/discussion, slide/discussion isn't critical. But there's no scenario under which you can run through forty-five slides in a one-hour meeting unless the meeting is going poorly.

You're probably thinking, *Guy's referring to the hoi polloi, great unwashed masses, and bozos. They should use only ten slides and twenty minutes, but not us. We have curve-jumping, paradigm-shifting, first-moving, patent-pending technology.*

I am, in fact, referring to *you.* I don't care if you sell dog food, permanent life, nano particles, optical components, or the cure for cancer: Ten slides and twenty minutes is all you get.

Thirty-Point–Font Text

This recommendation was originally intended for entrepreneurs pitching venture capitalists, but it applies to any meeting in which you

Investor Pitch (for both profits and not-for-profits)

SLIDE	CONTENT	COMMENTS
Title	Organization name; your name and title; and contact information.	The audience can read the slide—this is where you explain what your organization does. ("We sell software." "We sell hardware." "We are a school." "We are a church." "We protect the environment.") Cut to the chase!
Problem	Describe the pain that you're alleviating.The goal is to get everyone nodding and "buying in."	Avoid looking like a solution searching for a problem. Minimize or eliminate citations of consulting studies about the future size of your market.
Solution	Explain how you alleviate this pain and the meaning that you make. Ensure that the audience clearly understands what you sell and your value proposition.	This is not the place for an in-depth technical explanation. Provide just the gist of how you fix the pain—for example, "We are a discount travel Web site. We have written software that searches all other travel sites and collates their price quotes into one report."
Business Model	Explain how you make money: who pays you, your channels of distribution, and your gross margins.	Generally, a unique, untested business model is a scary proposition. If you truly have a revolutionary business model, explain it in terms of familiar ones. This is your opportunity to drop the names of the organizations that are already using your product or service.
Underlying Magic	Describe the technology, secret sauce, or magic behind your product or service.	The less text and the more diagrams, schematics, and flowcharts on this slide, the better. White papers and objective proofs of concepts are helpful here.

(continued)

Investor Pitch (for both profits and not-for-profits) *cont'd.*

SLIDE	CONTENT	COMMENTS
Marketing and Sales	Explain how you are going to reach your customer and your marketing leverage points.	Convince the audience that you have an effective go-to-market strategy that won't break the bank.
Competition	Provide a complete view of the competitive landscape. Too much is better than too little.	Never dismiss your competition. Everyone—customers, investors, employees—wants to hear why you're good, not why the competition is bad.
Management Team	Describe the key players of your management team, board of directors, and board of advisors, as well as your major investors.	Don't be afraid to show up with less than a perfect team. All startups have holes in their team—what's truly important is whether you understand that there are holes and are willing to fix them.
Financial Projections and Key Metrics	Provide a five-year forecast containing not only dollars but also key metrics, such as number of customers and conversion rate.	Do a bottom-up forecast (more about this in Chapter 5, "The Art of Bootstrapping"). Take into account long sales cycles and seasonality. Making people understand the underlying assumptions of your forecast is as important as the numbers you've fabricated.
Current Status, Accomplishments to Date, Timeline, and Use of Funds	Explain the current status of your product or service, what the near future looks like, and how you'll use the money you're trying to raise.	Share the details of your positive momemtum and traction. Then use this slide to close with a bias toward action.

Sales Prospect Pitch

SLIDE	CONTENT	COMMENTS
Title	Organization name; your name and title; and contact information.	The audience can read the slide—this is where you explain what your organization does. ("We sell software." "We sell hardware." "We are a school." "We are a church." "We protect the environment.") Cut to the chase!
Problem	Describe the customer pain that you're alleviating.	Be sure that you are sure that you're describing pain the customer has.
Solution	Explain how you alleviate this pain.	This is not the place for an in-depth technical explanation. Provide just the gist of how you fix the pain.
Sales Model	Ensure that the audience clearly understands what you sell and your value proposition.	This is your opportunity to drop the names of the organizations that are already buying your product or service. If you have a strong story in this area, add a slide called "Current Customers" instead of talking about it here.
Technology	Describe the technology, secret sauce, or magic behind your product or service.	The less text and the more diagrams, schematics, and flowcharts on this slide, the better. White papers and objective proofs of concepts are helpful here.
Demo	If possible, segue into a live demo of your product or service at this point.	A demo is worth a thousand slides if you can do a good one.

(continued)

Sales Prospect Pitch *cont'd.*

SLIDE	CONTENT	COMMENTS
Competitive Analysis	Provide a complete view of the competitive landscape. Too much is better than too little.	Find out in advance what competitive product or service the prospect uses. Even better, try to find out what problems the prospect is having with it. However, never dismiss your competition. Customers want to hear why you're good, not why the competition is bad.
Management Team	Describe the key players of your management team, board of directors, and board of advisors, as well as your major investors.	The purpose of doing this is to make the prospect feel comfortable with buying from a startup.
Next Steps	End your presentation with a call to action such as a trial period or a test installation.	

---

pitch your organization using a projector. Think about it: Any venture capitalist who survived the dotcom carnage is probably over forty and has deteriorating vision. A good rule of thumb for font size is to divide the oldest investor's age by two, and use that font size.

EXERCISE

Delete all the text that is smaller than fourteen points in your presentation. What remains is what your audience can read.

Seriously, if you have to use a small font to accommodate your material, you're putting too much detail on the slide. Each slide

Potential Partner Pitch

SLIDE	CONTENT	COMMENTS
Title	Organization name; your name and title; and contact information.	The audience can read the slide—this is where you explain what your organization does. ("We sell software." "We sell hardware." "We are a school." "We are a church." "We protect the environment.") Cut to the chase!
Problem	Describe the customer pain that you're alleviating.	Be sure that the potential partner currently sells, or wants to sell, to the same customer as you do.
Solution	Explain how you alleviate this pain for the customer, plus how you could do an even better job with a partnership.	The goal is to get the potential partner thinking how 2 + 2 can equal 5.
Partnership Model	Explain how the partnership would work: who does what, when, how, and why.	This slide should continue the positive effects of the previous slide—making the synergies more and more apparent and appealing.
Underlying Magic	Describe the technology, secret sauce, or magic behind your product or service.	The less text and the more diagrams, schematics, and flowcharts on this slide, the better. The purpose is to convince the potential partner that you have something special.
Demo	If possible, segue into a live demo of your product or service at this point.	Just like for customers, a demo is worth a thousand slides if you can do a good one.
Competition	This is an optional slide. The main reason to skip it is to avoid informing your potential partner of a better organization to work with than yours.	

(continued)

Potential Partner Pitch *cont'd.*

SLIDE	CONTENT	COMMENTS
Management Team	Describe the key players of your management team, board of directors, and board of advisors, as well as your major investors.	The purpose of doing this is to make the potential partner feel comfortable with working with a startup.
Next Steps	End your presentation with a call to action such as a trial period or a test installation.	

---

should portray one primary point. All the text and bullets should support this point.

Use slides to lead, not read. They should paraphrase and enhance what's coming out of your mouth. Because people can read faster than you talk, if you put too much detail on the slide, the audience will read ahead of you and not listen to what you're saying.

SET THE STAGE

If there's no projector when you show up for a meeting, it's your fault. If your laptop and the projector don't work together, it's your fault. If the bulb blows out in the middle of your pitch, it's your fault. If you start slowly, seem disorganized, and look disheveled, it's your fault.

It's almost impossible to recover from a bad start, so get there early and set the stage. Bring your own projector. Bring two laptops loaded up with your presentation. Bring a copy of your presentation on one of those USB-based flash memory products. Bring printouts of your presentation in case all hell breaks loose and nothing works.

The first words out of your mouth in the pitch should be

- "How much of your time may I have?" This question shows that you respect the value of the audience's time by not running over your limit.

- "What are the three most important things I can communicate to you?" (You should have gotten this in advance, but it doesn't hurt to clarify this again.)

- "May I quickly go through my PowerPoint presentation and handle questions at the end? However, please feel free to interrupt me if you need to."

If you set the stage so that everyone has the same expectations, you're way ahead of the game.

LET ONE PERSON DO THE TALKING

Entrepreneurs have it stuck in their heads that investors, customers, and partners want to work with teams, and teams show—guess what?—teamwork. Using this line of reasoning, they believe that four or five people from their organization should attend the meeting, and they should each have a role in the pitch because it shows how well the team works.

This logic is terrific for a school play: Every kid gets a talking role. Parents and grandparents get their photo opportunities. Everyone participates. Life is good, fair, and equitable. A pitch, however, is not a school play.

In a pitch, the CEO should do 80 percent of the talking. The rest of the team (and there should be no more than two others) can present the one or two slides pertaining to their specific area of expertise. They can also provide detailed answers if any questions arise. However, if the CEO can't handle most of the pitch by himself, he should practice until he can. Or, you should get a new CEO.

Often team members try to "rescue" the CEO when the audience pushes back on something he said. For example, suppose someone wants to debate a multiple-tier distribution system for selling products. A team member, with all good intentions, asserts, "I think you're right. I've thought for a long time that we should only sell directly to the customer."

Bad move. This doesn't show flexible thinking, an open environment, or a broad-based set of expertise. It shows a lack of cohesion.

The only right answer is for the CEO to say, "You raise a good point. Can we follow up with you on that?"

CATALYZE FANTASY

Every—literally *every*—entrepreneur shows up at Garage with a pitch that has three or four slides that "prove" the size of his market. Usually the slides contain a quote from a well-known consulting firm such as Gartner, IDG, or the Yankee Group stating unequivocally that the size of the "shrimp-farming software market will be $50 billion" within the next four years.

It's a funny thing about these slides:

- Every market is going to be at least $50 billion.
- The forecast is four to five years in the future. This time horizon is short enough to make the forecast believable, but long enough so that it is not provable.
- No one in the room, even the entrepreneur, believes the numbers or thinks they are particularly relevant.

There are two solutions to this problem. The first is to start with the $50 billion number and peel away the layers of the onion until you arrive at the realistic "total addressable market" (TAM). The TAM is the true size of the potential market you can go after, not the totality of every nickel that's spent in something related to your product or service.

For example, the TAM of a new sushi bar is not the $50 billion spent every year by Americans eating out. Nor is it the $5 billion spent on ethnic food. It's the $1 million spent on Japanese food within fifty miles of your prospective location.

The advantage of taking this approach is that it shows that you truly understand the makeup of the market, and that you are realistic in what segments you can address. This builds your credibility for the rest of the pitch—while quite the opposite occurs if you insist that the market is $50 billion.

The second solution is bolder: Forget the market research and catalyze fantasy. You do this by providing a product or service that is so obviously needed that members of your audience can do the math in their heads. This method won't work in all cases because some markets are not that obvious, but when it does work, it is spectacular.

Here is an example of how it can work. Suppose you make a product that tests the security of Web sites that accept text input from visitors. Your product ensures that hackers cannot penetrate your site through these input fields.

Here's how the fantasy would go:

- Almost every Web site has a place to enter text.
- There are a lot of Web sites.
- Every company is afraid of being hacked into.
- Lots of companies will need to buy this product.

This line of fantasy is much more powerful than citing a study that proves the market for security software will be "$50 billion in four years" because the audience has heard four other pitches that day with numbers just as big. And those pitches were for shrimp-farming software, wireless access points, nano particles, and graphics chips.

GET TO ONE THOUSAND FEET AND STAY THERE

I promise that this is the only war analogy in this book. Consider three methods to deliver lethal force:

- **B-1B LANCER.** This is a long-range bomber for intercontinental missions that is capable of penetrating sophisticated defense systems. It can fly up to thirty thousand feet above the ground. It costs $200 million.

- **NAVY SEALS.** They are part of the U.S. Navy. They are trained for special operations in enemy territory. They provide unconventional warfare capabilities and real-time eyes on targets by striking from, and returning to, the sea.

- **A-10 WARTHOG.** This plane was designed for close air support of troops. It is simple and rugged. Its sweet spot is flying at one thousand feet. It costs $13 million.

If pitches were weapons, the majority would be B-1 Lancers or Navy Seals. The B-1 pitch is up in the clouds. It features a lot of hand-waving, cool PowerPoint animations, and use of terms such as *strategic, partnerships, alliances, first-mover advantage,* and *patented technology.* Typically, it's delivered by an MBA with a finance or consulting background.

Geeks, propeller heads, and engineers deliver the Navy Seal pitch. They explain the subtle nuances of their technology and use a lot of acronyms that only they understand. It's clear that these people know every bit of their technology—and would love to explain it all to you.

The B-1 pitch is too high because listeners want to learn specifically what the business does and why it will succeed. Big words don't accomplish this. The Navy Seal pitch is too low because it focuses on the bits, bytes, and nits. But a pitch isn't about microscopic due diligence.

The right analogy for pitching your business is neither the B-1 Lancer (30,000 feet) nor the Navy Seal (0 feet). It's the A-10 Warthog (1,000 feet). Like the plane itself, your pitch doesn't have to be pretty, just effective: above the ground but still tactical.

Pitch at the thousand-foot level. Up there you're not above the clouds where the air is thin, but you're not on the ground with a knife in your teeth, either. Provide enough detail to prove you can deliver and enough aerial view to prove you have a vision.

SHUT UP, TAKE NOTES, SUMMARIZE, REGURGITATE, AND FOLLOW UP

There are very few people who don't become more interesting when they stop talking.

—Mary Lowry

I once accompanied a startup's CEO and COO on a pitch to a venture capitalist. A few days after the pitch, I met with the venture capitalist alone. When we began to discuss the Management (with a capital *M*), all he said was, "I noticed that the CEO did a lot of talking, but the COO was sitting there taking notes. The CEO didn't write down a thing. I think the COO is a quality guy."

I don't remember whether what the venture capitalist had been saying at the original meeting was actually noteworthy, but that's not the point. The point is that shutting up and taking notes or, God help you, actually listening for ways to improve is a good thing to do in a pitch, where even the smallest actions create a big impression. The visible act of taking notes says

- I think you're smart.
- You're saying something worth writing down.
- I'm willing and anxious to learn.
- I'm conscientious.

Taking notes provides these benefits, plus the value of the information that you're recording. It can't get much better than this.

Also, at the end of the meeting, summarize what you heard and play it back in order to make sure you got the correct information. You can make an even greater impression by also following through, within a day, on all the promises that you made during the pitch—for example, providing additional information.

REWRITE FROM SCRATCH

This is a difficult recommendation for people to accept, but first, allow me to digress briefly and tell you about cars in the Philippines. Because of import duties, restrictions on trade, and the low cost of labor, fixing cars there is a much more attractive proposition than buying new ones.

Thus, many cars are rebuilt and patched with parts cannibalized from other vehicles, as well as with handmade components. For example, it's common to see a Jeep with a Chevrolet engine.

Unfortunately, after a while, many pitches start looking like these cars. They started as one model, but their owners kept editing and patching them after each meeting in response to the most recent questions and objections.

This process goes on for weeks—with each meeting producing more edits, fixes, and patches—until it's difficult to recognize the pitch at all, which by this point touches upon every subject but obfuscates the overall message.

Here's my recommendation: After ten or so pitches, throw away your presentation. Start with a clean slate and write the text from scratch. Let this "version 2.0" reflect the gestalt of what you've learned to date instead of being a patchwork quilt.

PITCH CONSTANTLY

Familiarity breeds content. It's when you are totally familiar and comfortable with your pitch that you'll be able to give it most effectively. There are no shortcuts to achieving familiarity—you simply have to pitch a lot of times.

Twenty-five times is what it takes for most people to reach this point. All these pitches don't have to be to your intended audiences—your co-founders, employees, relatives, friends, and even your dog are fine auditors.

Forget the theory of "rising to the occasion" when you actually give the pitch. If you're lousy in practice, you'll be lousy in the pitch, so get going—because if there's anything worse than getting tinnitus, it's causing it.

> **EXERCISE**
> Videotape yourself giving your pitch. If you can watch it without being embarrassed, you're ready to go.

MINICHAPTER: THE ART OF POWERPOINTING

In some cases . . . the knife can turn savagely upon the person wielding it. . . . You use the knife carefully, because you know it doesn't care who it cuts.

—Stephen King

PowerPoint is a Swiss Army knife for entrepreneurs. It started off as a tool and has become an end in itself—cluttering the effectiveness of most pitches. Before you cut yourself, heed this advice about the art of using PowerPoint as a means to an end.

- **USE A DARK BACKGROUND.** A dark background communicates seriousness and substance. A white or light background looks cheap and amateurish. Also, staring at a harsh white presentation for forty-five minutes gets tiring for the eyes. Think about this: Have you ever seen movie credits that use black text on a white background?

- **ADD YOUR LOGO TO THE MASTER PAGE.** Every presentation is a chance to build brand awareness for your organization, so put your logo on the master slide page. By doing this, your logo will appear on every slide.

- **USE COMMON, SANS SERIF FONTS.** A presentation is not the place to show that you've accumulated the world's largest collection of fonts. Use common fonts because someday your presentation may need to be given on a computer that has a different collection of fonts than your computer has. Also, use sans serif fonts because they are much easier to read than the delicate serif font you love. You can never go wrong with Arial.

- **ANIMATE YOUR BODY, NOT YOUR SLIDES.** PowerPoint has more than sixty ways to animate text and graphics. This is about fifty-nine too many. Many entrepreneurs use animations and transitions between slides to jazz up their presentations. Do you really think that a "faded fly-in from the bottom left" is going to make a presentation better? Do yourself a favor: Don't use fancy animations. Use your body, not PowerPoint, to communicate expressiveness, emotion, and enthusiasm. Generally speaking, if you think something is cool, cut it.

- **"BUILD" BULLETS.** Most entrepreneurs don't use bullets. They display and read big blocks of long text. That's a mistake. Use bullets instead: short bursts of text that capture the main point. Even when entrepreneurs use bullets, they put them all up at once. That's also a mistake. Build your bullets: click, bullet 1, explain; click, bullet 2, explain; click, bullet 3, explain. This is the only time you should use animation, and I recommend using the simple "appear" animation at that.

- **USE ONLY ONE LEVEL OF BULLETS.** The use of bullets with bullets means that you're trying to communicate too much information on a slide or that your thinking is fuzzy. Each slide should communicate one point, with bullets to support that point. If you observe the 30 part of the 10/20/30 rule, it will be hard to have bullets with bullets, anyway.

- **ADD DIAGRAMS AND GRAPHS.** Better a bullet than a block of text, but better a diagram or graph than a bullet. Use diagrams to explain how your business works. Use graphs to explain trends and numerical results. And build your diagrams and pictures by bringing in these elements with clicks, just like bullets.

- **MAKE PRINTABLE SLIDES.** There is a cautionary aspect to adding diagrams and graphics. Sometimes these objects build upon, and cover, previous ones. This is okay during a presentation but not when printed, so ensure that your slides work for this use, too.

FAQ

Q. How do I make my pitch memorable?

A. The problem is not that pitches are boring. In a vacuum, many are quite exciting, what with their promises of first-mover advantage, patented technology, $50 billion market, and proven teams of highly motivated geniuses.

The problem is that so many pitches sound alike because they all make the same claims. You can make yours memorable by preparing a short (ten-slide, twenty-minute) presentation with a compelling story of how you solve real pain. Less than 1 percent of pitches do this.

To develop a memorable pitch, imagine that your audience is at the end of a long day of boring meetings; everyone is barely awake, much less attentive; and people just want to go home. More often than not, this is what you'll walk into, so be prepared for it.

Q. Should I send my presentation in advance to the attendees?

A. No. A good presentation typically features only snippets of text (in a big font!), so recipients will most likely find it difficult to comprehend without your riveting oral presentation.

Q. Should I hand out my presentation at the start of the meeting?

A. I wouldn't. My theory is that if you do this at the beginning, people will skip ahead because they can read faster than you can talk. However, this makes it more difficult for the audience to take notes. An alternative strategy is to hand out the presentation at the start of the meeting, but ask people not to skip ahead.

RECOMMENDED READING

Borden, Richard. *Public Speaking—as Listeners Like It!* New York: Harper & Brothers, 1935. (Also recommended in Chapter 9, "The Art of Branding," this book is seriously out of print, but I found a copy at Amazon.com.)

Piattelli-Palmarini, Massimo. *Inevitable Illusions: How Mistakes of Reason Rule Our Minds.* New York: John Wiley & Sons, 1994.

CHAPTER 4

The Art of Writing a Business Plan

In preparing for battle I have always found that plans are useless, but planning is indispensable.

—Dwight D. Eisenhower

GIST

According to Celtic myths, there were once magical vessels that "satisfied the tastes and needs of all who ate and drank from them."* These myths led to the legend of the Holy Grail. The modern-day equivalent of the Holy Grail is the business plan.

It, too, is supposed to satisfy everyone (investors, directors, founders, and managers) and induce magical effects on those who partake of it—specifically, the irresistible urge to write a check or approve a go-ahead action.

Also, like the Holy Grail, the business plan remains largely unattainable and mythological. Most experts wouldn't agree, but a business plan is of limited usefulness for a startup because entrepreneurs base so much of their plans on assumptions, "visions," and unknowns.

*Found at http://www.bl.uk/whatson/exhibitions/grail.html.

An entrepreneurial endeavor within an existing company will also find that a business plan is of limited use. For external and internal startups, the MAT (Milestones, Assumptions, and Tasks) that we discussed in Chapter 1 is the most useful guide for the day-to-day operation of an organization.

However, many investors, recruits, potential board members, and internal decision makers do expect a business plan and won't proceed without one. Plus, writing a business plan does have the benefit of forcing a team to work together to formalize intentions. So write a plan, and write it well, but don't convince yourself that it's the Holy Grail. Organizations are successful because of good implementation, not good business plans.

WRITE FOR THE RIGHT REASON

Ironically, for most entrepreneurs the business plan itself (that is, the document) is one of the least important factors in raising money.

- If an investor is leaning toward a positive decision, then the business plan only reinforces this inkling. It probably wasn't responsible for the positive position itself.

- If the investor is leaning toward a negative decision, then it's unlikely that the plan will change his mind. In this case, the investor probably won't even read the entire plan.

Unfortunately, naïve entrepreneurs believe that a business plan alone can produce an awestruck reaction, followed by one follow-up question: "Can you send me wiring instructions for the money?"

Dream on. The right and realistic reasons to write a business plan are

- In the later, due-diligence stage of courting an investor, the investor will ask for one. It's part of the game—a business plan has to be "in the file."

- Writing a plan forces the founding team to work together. With any luck, this will help generate a strong, cohesive team. You might even figure out whom you *don't* want to work with.

- Writing a plan makes the team consider issues that it had over-looked or glossed over in its euphoria—for example, developing a customer service policy.

- Finally, the writing of a plan uncovers holes in the founding team. If you look around the room and realize that no one can implement key elements of the plan, you know that someone is missing.

All the late-night, back-o'-the-envelope, romantic intentions to change the world become tangible and debatable once they're put on paper. Thus, the document itself is not nearly as important as the process that leads to the document. Even if you aren't trying to raise money, you should write one anyway.

PITCH, THEN PLAN

Many entrepreneurs try to perfect their business plan and then pull PowerPoint slides out of it. They view the business plan as the be-all and end-all, and the pitch as a subset of this magnificent document.

This is backward thinking. A good business plan is a detailed version of a pitch—as opposed to a pitch being a distilled version of a business plan. If you get the pitch right, you'll get the plan right. The converse is not true. Here's the proper process:

- Throw together a pitch that contains the ten slides we discussed in the previous chapter.
- Try it out on some mentors, colleagues, relatives, angels, and investors. Do this about ten times.
- Get the team in a room and discuss what you've learned.
- Fix the pitch.
- Start writing the plan.

Here's why this is the right methodology to writing a plan:

- Your pitch is more important than your business plan, as it will determine whether you're rejected or generate further interest. Few sophisticated investors will read a business plan as the first step.

- A pitch is easier to fix than a business plan because it contains less text.

- You won't get feedback on your business plan. Frankly, it may not even be read. You will, however, get immediate reactions to your pitch.

- You may get lucky and raise money without ever having to write a business plan. (But I would still write one for the value of the process.)

FOCUS ON THE EXECUTIVE SUMMARY

As a refresher, these are the ten slides that are necessary in a good pitch for investors:

1. Title slide
2. Problem
3. Solution
4. Business model
5. Underlying magic
6. Marketing and sales
7. Competition
8. Management team
9. Financial projections and key metrics
10. Current status, accomplishments to date, timeline, and use of funds

These ten items provide the framework for your business plan as well. An executive summary takes the place of the title slide and is the most important part of the plan. A good executive summary is a concise and clear description of the problem you solve, how you solve it, your business model, and the underlying magic of your product or service. It should be approximately four paragraphs in length.

It is the most important part of your business plan because it will determine whether people read the rest of the document. If all goes well, they'll ask you to come in for a meeting. However, if the executive summary fails to spark interest, then the game is lost before it even begins, and the rest of the business plan won't matter because no one will ever get to it.

Thus, of the effort you put into writing a business plan, 80 percent should go into the executive summary. These are the most important paragraphs of your organization's existence.

EXERCISE

Print your current business plan. Throw away page 3 and beyond. Would the first two pages make you want to read the whole document?

KEEP IT CLEAN

In addition to writing a great executive summary, you can increase the effectiveness of your entire business plan by keeping it short, simple, and effective:

- **DO NOT EXCEED TWENTY PAGES IN LENGTH.** You're probably thinking that this principle is only relevant to other people's plans, and that your own curve-jumping, revolutionary organization is the exception to the rule. You're wrong. The shorter the plan, the more likely it is to be read.

- **SELECT ONE PERSON TO WRITE THE BUSINESS PLAN.** While the plan should reflect the wisdom of the team, it should be articulated by a single voice. It should not read like a patchwork of cutting and pasting.

- **BIND THE PLAN WITH A STAPLE.** Leather-bound, gold-leaf, embossed tomes make you stand out—but as a clueless bozo. Investors will probably ask for a Word document or PDF electronically transmitted copy anyway.

- **SIMPLIFY YOUR FINANCIAL PROJECTIONS TO TWO PAGES.** Investors don't care—and you have no way of knowing—how much you'll spend for pencils in the eleventh month of the fourth year. The most important projection is your cash flow statement for the first five years. (See the next section for more information about financial projections.)

- **INCLUDE THE KEY METRICS, SUCH AS THE NUMBER OF CUS-TOMERS, LOCATIONS, AND RESELLERS.** Often these metrics provide a better understanding of an organization's plans than financial projections. For example, you may project that you'll sell to 250 of the *Fortune* 500 companies in the first year.

- **INCLUDE THE ASSUMPTIONS THAT DRIVE YOUR FINANCIAL PROJECTIONS.** Everyone knows that you picked a revenue number that you think makes your business look interesting but not hallucinatory. The assumptions behind your forecast are much more informative and important than the forecast itself.

PROVIDE THE RIGHT NUMBERS

Investors don't spread business plans across the table and pick the ones to fund based solely on financial projections. Most business plans submitted to venture capitalists are more similar than they are different. Specifically, they all project fourth- or fifth-year sales of $25 million to $50 million. Anyone who can boot Excel can achieve these theoretical results.

However, financial projections, which investors require, are a significant part of a business plan. Generally, they want five years of projections to help them understand the scale of your business, determine how much capital you'll require, and consider the assumptions inherent in your business model. Here is how four leading venture capitalists describe what they look for in financial projections.

> **HEIDI ROIZEN (MOBIUS VENTURE CAPITAL):** "I like to see detailed monthly numbers for the whole use of the round of capital in question, then quarterly for the year after that, then annual through profitability, which I realize are fantasy but I want to understand the assumptions the entrepreneur is using to get to total market, total share they will get, and what it will cost to get there."

> **MIKE MORITZ (SEQUOIA CAPITAL):** "No projections ever come true, so entrepreneurs should forget about trying to assemble a compendious set of financials. An early-stage venture capital investor really just

wants to gauge how much money is going to be required until the company can support itself from its own cash flow. We always focus on the first eighteen months to two years on the assumption that if we can weather this period we will be in far better shape to deal with what comes after. We like a few well–thought-out projections (by quarter for the first two years and annually for years 3, 4, and 5) that present a profit-and-loss statement, a balance sheet, and cash flow projections."

GARY SHAFFER (MORGENTHALER VENTURES): "Five years is typical, despite the typical lack of credibility of the further-out years. A shorter time frame, like three years, may be fine for raw startups. As a rule of thumb, investors are typically looking for a forecast that goes out to whatever year is necessary for the company to get to 'significant' revenues. And if that's more than five years, that might be appropriate. That helps bracket how much cash will be required to finance the company to profitability, which is something investors always want to have a rough idea about."

STEVE JURVETSON (DRAPER, FISHER, JURVETSON): "Every business plan has financial projections that start low and shoot up to absurdly high profit forecasts for the third year. We typically discount these projections, but the forecast is useful to show optimism and growth potential. What's more important than the projection, however, are the assumptions used to reach the conclusions: the business model, the market size, the pricing, channels and resulting gross margins, and the capital intensity needed to fund growth. Ultimately, we want to fund entrepreneurs who want to change the world, and to initiate those discussions, a half-page of five-year financial projections coupled with a thoughtful discussion of the key drivers should suffice."

WRITE DELIBERATE, ACT EMERGENT

In *The Innovator's Solution* coauthors Clayton Christensen and Michael E. Raynor explain the difference between a "deliberate strategy-making process" and an "emergent strategy-making process." The former is "conscious and analytical," featuring rigorous use of historical data, technology road maps, and competitive analysis. It is useful for mature companies with operating histories.*

By contrast, an emergent strategy-making process is influenced by the day-to-day realities experienced by middle managers and workers on the front line. It is ad hoc and can react quickly to problems and opportunities. This is the right process to use in situations where the future is murky, and it's therefore difficult to develop suitable strategies.† It is appropriate for startups, and for startups within mature companies.

Here's the dirty little secret of business plans for startups: You should write them in the "deliberate" style, but you should be thinking and acting in the "emergent" style. Investors want deliberate plans because they want to invest in companies that supposedly know what they are doing. Most of them will not find "we'll react fast" to be a palatable strategy.

You and I both know that you don't know when your product or service will ship, who will buy it, how much they will pay, and if they'll ever reorder it, but you can't state this in a business plan. So write as if you know exactly what the future holds, but react opportunistically when you encounter reality.

Rest assured that many successful organizations have changed their business models along the way. This means you have to conserve your capital so you have money to make it through the changes (hence Chapter 5 on bootstrapping later in this book), and you have to be willing to alter your plans.

The worst thing to do is to write a deliberate plan and then stick to it simply because it is "the plan." If you're successful, no one will care if you didn't follow the plan. And shame on you if you fail but you did.

---

*Clayton Christensen and Michael E. Raynor, *The Innovator's Solution* (Boston: Harvard Business School Press, 2003), 214.
†Ibid., 215

FAQ

Q. Won't my business plan look pretty much like everyone else's?

A. This depends on what you mean by "look like everyone else's." In one sense, it *should* look like other plans. That is, it should contain the essential topics mentioned earlier in this chapter. Furthermore, it should not have an unusual layout, design, or binding—much less your color picture on the cover. Arial font for headings and Palatino font for text are just fine.

Q. OK, then how do I make my plan stand out?

A. There are four ways to make your plan stand out. First, have a credible referral source bring it to the attention of the reader. Second, provide a list of customers the reader can call to discuss how much they need your product or service—or, even better, how much they are *already* using your product or service. Third, ensure that the plan is infused with real-world knowledge about and experience with the market. Fourth, include diagrams and graphics to explain complex points.

Q. Is it better to write the plan myself or use a consultant? How about a consultant just for the financial model?

A. You, or your team and you, should write the entire plan, including building the financial model. As I mentioned above, the most important outcome of the business plan process is getting the founding team, no pun intended, on the same page. If you abdicate any part of the process, you're making a big mistake. After you write the plan, you can use a consultant to review what you've done.

Q. How often should I review the business plan?

A. The usefulness of a business plan rapidly declines after the first six months or so. Initially, a business plan gets the team on the same page, helps get new employees up to speed, and raises money.

However, from the second year on, you won't be writing emergent plans. At that point, your business plan will be deliberate: focusing on budgeting and forecasting with quick summarizations of goals (what) and strategies (how).

RECOMMENDED READING

Christensen, Clayton, and Michael E. Raynor. *The Innovator's Solution: Creating and Sustaining Successful Growth*. Boston: Harvard Business School Press, 2003

Nesheim, John. *High Tech Startup: The Complete Handbook for Creating Successful New High-Tech Companies*. New York: Free Press, 2000.

Trout, Jack. *The Power of Simplicity: A Management Guide to Cutting Through the Nonsense and Doing Things Right*. New York: McGraw-Hill, 1999.

Activation

CHAPTER 5

The Art of Bootstrapping

It's all right to aim high if you have plenty of ammunition.
—Hawley R. Everhart

GIST

B ill Reichert, a managing director of Garage, likes to tell entrepreneurs that the odds of raising venture capital are equal to the odds of getting struck by lightning while standing on the bottom of a swimming pool on a sunny day. He's exaggerating. The odds aren't that good.

Most entrepreneurs have to dig, scratch, and claw out a business while living on soy sauce and rice. This chapter explains how to survive the critical, capital-deprived early days of any startup's existence by picking the right business model, making cash king, immediately getting to market, and taking the "red pill."

Incidentally, some people think that a bootstrappable business must by its very nature be a trivial one—that is, if you keep capital requirements low and can't raise wheelbarrows full of venture capital, you've limited yourself to something small. They are wrong. Companies such as Hewlett-Packard, Dell, Microsoft, Apple, and eBay all started with a bootstrap model.

If you plan carefully, bootstrapping will only be a stage in your business's development. It doesn't have to be your permanent lifestyle—because after a while, soy sauce and rice do get boring. But for the time being, think big and start small.

MANAGE FOR CASH FLOW, NOT PROFITABILITY

In the early days of The New Yorker, *the offices were so small and sparsely furnished that Dorothy Parker preferred to spend her days at a nearby coffee shop. One day, the editor found her sitting there.*
"Why aren't you upstairs, working?" demanded Harold Ross.
"Someone was using the pencil," Mrs. Parker explained. *

Entrepreneurs can bootstrap almost any business—especially if they have no choice in the matter. I may never be invited to speak at a business school again for saying so, but a bootstrappable business model means managing for cash flow, not "paper" profits, growth, market share, or branding.

A bootstrappable business model has many of the following characteristics:

- low up-front capital requirements
- short (under a month) sales cycles
- short (under a month) payment terms
- recurring revenue
- word-of-mouth advertising

On the revenue side, managing for cash flow means passing up sales that are profitable but take a long time to collect. On the expense side, it means stretching out payments for everything you buy.

On paper, your organization will appear to be less profitable—primarily because of the foregone sales. However, paper profits are a secondary consideration for a bootstrapper.

*Peter Hay, *The Book of Business Anecdotes* (New York: Wings Books, 1988), 149.

These requirements point to products, services, and target markets with the following characteristics:

- People already know, or it becomes immediately obvious, that they need your product or service. You don't have to educate your potential customers about their pain.

- Your product or service is "auto-persuasive."* That is, once people recognize their pain and how you solve it, they can persuade themselves to take the next step and buy what you're offering.

- A megatrend tsunami of a market is breaking down barriers for you. The Internet was an example of this. (Realize, however, that every wave eventually runs out of energy, so you must have a "real business" by the time that happens.)

- You can piggyback on a product or service that already has a large installed base. You reduce risk by betting on another product or service that is already successful.

Managing for cash flow, not profitability, isn't a long-term practice, but until you are sitting on a pile of cash, it's the way to go for a bootstrapper.

BUILD A BOTTOM-UP FORECAST

No bootstrapper in his right mind would do a top-down forecast by calculating how much of a market one needs to be successful. This is the kind of model that typically starts with a large number and works down to extrapolate projected sales from that figure. For example, let's say you're starting a company to sell Internet access in China. Here's a typical top-down model:

- There are 1.3 billion people.
- 1 percent want Internet access.
- We'll get 10 percent of that potential audience.

*Michael Schrage, "Letting Buyers Sell Themselves," *Technology Review* (October 2003): 17.

- Each account will yield $240 per year.
- 1.3 billion people × 1% addressable market × 10% success rate × $240/customer = $312 million. And—added bonus!—look at how conservative these percentages are!

If you pick a big enough market, it's easy to fool yourself into thinking success won't be hard to achieve. One percent, for example, always seems like a small, easily attained market share.

Bootstrappers don't build top-down models. For them, top down = belly up! Instead, they build bottom-up models, starting with real-world variables such as

- Each salesperson can make ten phone sales calls a day that get through to a prospect.
- There are 240 working days per year.
- Five percent of the sales calls will convert within six months.
- Each successful sale will bring in $240 worth of business.
- We can bring on board five salespeople.
- Ten calls/day × 240 days/year × 5% success rate × $240/sale × 5 salespeople = $144,000 in sales in the first year.

You can argue as much as you like about the precise number of calls per day, success rate, average sale, etc.; the point here is that a bottom-up model yields a much more realistic forecast than even the most pessimistic market share estimates of a consultant's forecast about the total size of a market.

The magnitude of your bottom-up forecast will establish the degree of bootstrapping you'll have to do. The only information that will point out the need for bootstrapping more accurately is looking at your bank account balance.

SHIP, THEN TEST

If you're starting a biotech or medical device company, ignore this section. All others, read on. One of the hallmarks of bootstrapping is to get your product or service immediately to market. Think this way:

Ship, fix, ship, fix, ship, fix, ship . . . instead of fix, fix, fix, ship. Admittedly, there are pros and cons to this philosophy.

PROS
- immediate cash flow
- real-world feedback

CONS
- tarnished image if there are quality problems

Because a tarnished image is potentially a big negative, there's always a god-awful tension involved in deciding between shipping and perfecting. Here are some questions to consider as you make this decision:

- Does our product or service, at this stage of development, leapfrog the competition?
- Can we ship it into a geographic area or market segment that is small and isolated, so that potential damage is limited?
- Is there a tolerant and understanding customer or group of customers who are willing to be guinea pigs?
- Does our product or service largely fulfill our vision for making meaning?
- Does it largely fill the needs of our customers?
- Can the current state of our product or service endanger or do harm to the customer?
- Have we already done so much "in vitro" testing that we need to know what the real world thinks?

EXERCISE

True or false? The first Macintosh (1984) did not have software, hard disks, slots, color, and Ethernet.

You can spend hours discussing these questions with your team. It won't be easy to reach a conclusion, and there is no "right" or "wrong" answer. Another way you can approach this dilemma is to ask yourself, *Would I let my mother or father use the product or service in its current state?* If the answer is yes, ship it.

Another question you could pose is this: *Are we running out of money?* Nothing can focus an organization like the prospect of death.

FORGET THE "PROVEN" TEAM

Experience is the name everyone gives to their mistakes.

—Oscar Wilde

If you're bootstrapping your organization, forget about recruiting the well-known industry veterans and building a dream team. Focus, instead, on affordability—that is, inexperienced young people with bushels of raw talent and energy.

This will initially reduce the prospects of raising venture capital, but standing on the bottom of a swimming pool isn't that enjoyable anyway. Besides, the following table shows how easy it is to build a case for unproven people.

	PROVEN PEOPLE	UNPROVEN PEOPLE
Salary	High, but you don't always get what you paid for	Low, and you almost always get at least what you paid for
Perks	Secretaries, nice hotels, first-class travel, limos, and top-of-the-line equipment	Self-service, motels, coach class, car pools, and equipment bought at auctions
Energy Level	Still high, ideally	Controllable, ideally
Knowledge	Don't admit what they don't know, but you assume they know everything	Don't know what they don't know, so they're willing to try anything

Of these factors, the last one is the most important: Ignorance is not only bliss, it's empowering. Back in the eighties (when I was young), I didn't know how hard it would be to evangelize a new operating system, so when Apple offered me a job, I jumped at it—it was like being paid to go to Disneyland. Post-Macintosh, I know how hard it is, and I would never try to do it again. Had I not been empowered by ignorance of the "impossibility" of my task, I would never have attempted it.

EXERCISE

Go on the Internet and investigate the backgrounds of the following entrepreneurs:

Bill Gates	David Filo
Steve Jobs	Larry Page
Michael Dell	Sergei Brin
Pierre Omidyar	Oprah Winfrey
Jerry Yang	Anita Roddick

You will see that "on paper," none of them had the "right" background to create a multibillion-dollar company.

START AS A SERVICE BUSINESS

One of the advantages of a service business is that cash starts flowing immediately. The classic example of this form of bootstrapping is a software company. The fairy tale goes like this:

- Some programmers get together to provide services to a niche market. They operate as consultants—getting down and dirty with the client. Billing is on an hourly basis and payable within thirty days.

- In the course of providing this service, they develop a software tool for the client. As they add clients, they continue to enhance the tool. Soon, they realize that there are many customers who can use this tool.

- They use the consulting fees from clients to fund further development of the tool. At this point, the consulting practice has grown and provides a steady base of profits.

- They complete development of the tool and try to sell it independent of consulting services. Sales take off. The company stops doing consulting because "there's no leverage in consulting."

- The company goes public, or Microsoft acquires it. The founders buy Porsches, Audis, or Mercedes and live happily ever after.

Another way, slightly grimmer, that companies adopt the service model goes like this:

- A couple of guys have an idea for a software company. They are going to put Oracle, Microsoft, or Symantec out of business.

- They start creating the product. Maybe they raise venture capital. Maybe they raise angel capital. Maybe they just starve.

- For the first time in the history of mankind, development takes longer than the entrepreneurs expected. Also, customers aren't willing to buy the product from two guys in a garage. The company is running out of money.

- To get some cash flowing, the guys decide that they should do some consulting. They take their partially finished product and pound the pavement looking for any business they can find. They rationalize this decision as a positive step because it helps them develop a product that customers truly need.

- Lo and behold, customers really do need their product. The developers complete it and start selling it. Sales take off, and they stop doing consulting because "there's no leverage in consulting."

- The company goes public, or Microsoft acquires it. The founders buy Porsches, Audis, or Mercedes and live happily ever after.

Whether the path your company takes is the fairy tale or the grim fairy tale doesn't really matter, if you pull it off. The message is that starting (or being driven to) a service model is a viable bootstrapping technique.

If you do take this path, however, understand that starting as a service business is a good initial path but isn't always the right long-term strategy. Getting customers to pay for your research and development should be only a temporary strategy for a product-based company.

In the long run, a service business is fundamentally different from a product business. The former is all about slave labor and billable hours or projects. The latter is all about research and development, shipping, and spreading costs over thousands of boxes going out the door.

FOCUS ON FUNCTION, NOT FORM

When spending money, always focus on the function you need, not the form it takes. For example, proper accounting does not mean retaining a big-name firm (form) and then assuming the job will get done (function). What's important is the function, not the form (see the following table).

Service providers are a big part of startup costs, so here are tips on making the right choice when assessing them:

- Select a firm that specializes in the type of work that you require. For example, to review venture capital finance work, you should not hire Uncle Joe the divorce lawyer because he's cheaper, or a Wall Street law firm simply because it has a big name.

- Understand that at times the right decision will be to pay more. Investors, for example, may feel more comfortable dealing with companies that use the "usual" lawyers and accountants who do your type of work.

- Check the references of the individuals who are handling your business—and not just "the firm's." The most powerful reference these providers can have is happy entrepreneurs.

- Negotiate everything. Circa 2004, *everything* is negotiable: rates, payment schedules, and monthly fees. Even in good times, don't be

	FORM	FUNCTION
Legal	Offices around the world for a *Fortune* 500 clientele and box seats at sporting events.	Understanding your legal liabilities, protecting your assets, and facilitating deals.
Accounting	Big-Six status with former clients in jail and walnut walls in conference rooms.	Controlling costs and ensuring fiscally sound operation.
PR	Good-looking account reps who majored in Asian art history and who tell you that you're a great speaker are at the $100,000 press event they planned.	Creating and proselytizing effective positioning and establishing close contacts with the press.
Advertising	A wall full of awards for television commercials and print ads with employees who do nothing but buy media.	Understanding and reaching your customer and getting current customers to attract future customers.
Headhunting	Established reputation for placing the CEOs of publicly traded companies that own private jets.	Hiring great employees who will trade options for salary.

afraid to negotiate—it's part of the game. Many firms, for example, will delay billing until you're funded if you have the chutzpah to ask.

- If you can't stand the person you'll be working with, switch people or switch firms. Life is short, so work with vendors you like.

This logic of focusing on function, not form, applies to almost every element of a startup organization. One of the symbols of the dotcom craze, for example, was the Herman Miller Aeron chair. This was a $700 piece of office equipment that was the de rigueur indicator of cool during the period. It was a terrific chair, but I don't know if it was $700 terrific. The function of a chair, after all, is to support one's butt.

> **EXERCISE**
> Go to eBay and search for used Aeron chairs. The more you find, the more it means that entrepreneurs focused on form, not function.

PICK YOUR BATTLES

Whisper the word *commodity* to most entrepreneurs, and you'll send shivers up their spines. The term has come to mean the process by which a product that was once unique and proprietary and that commanded high margins has become commonplace, standardized, and cheap.

However, bootstrapping startups love it when products become commodities, because their cost of goods sold decreases. For example, Neoteris, the Sunnyvale, California, provider of networking security devices, sells its product for $10,000. The cost of parts is only $2,000.*

If Neoteris were to design and manufacture the parts for its product, the cost and risks would be much greater. By buying off-the-shelf parts from larger businesses, the company is tapping into the resources of industry giants such as Intel.

Bootstrappers pick their battles. The battle for Neoteris, and where it makes its money, is in writing software—not designing and manufacturing chips or hard disks. Don't try to make money doing the things anyone can do. Make money from your magic:

- What is the crucial "magic" that we're creating?
- Are customers buying from us because of the "parts" in our product or service—or because of how we integrate them to create a solution?
- How can we tap into the efforts of other organizations to get to market better, faster, and cheaper?
- How many processes can we do well? Are there other organizations that can do them better for us?

GO DIRECT

Many startup organizations try to implement a multiple-tiered distribution system. That is, the company sells to a reseller, who then sells

*Om Malik, "The Rise of the Instant Company," *Business 2.0* (December 2003): 99.

to the final user of the product or service. The thinking here is that an established reseller/consultant/distributor brings the benefits of a sales force, brand awareness, and preexisting customer relationships.

That's the theory, anyway. It usually breaks down because most resellers want to fill demand, not create it. They're not interested in helping you establish a market—they simply want to tap into a proven one. Marxist (Groucho) as this may seem, you wouldn't want any reseller that would have you.

There are three additional issues to be weighed when considering a multiple-tiered distribution system. First, it isolates you from your customer. With a new product or service, you need to hear what's wrong and what's right as soon as possible and as unfiltered as possible. Second, because there's much less profit margin, you need to generate a large volume of sales, and it's usually difficult to achieve large volume as a startup. Finally, it takes a long time to both set up a distribution system and get your product through the system into the hands of customers.

For all these reasons, sell directly to customers. Once you've debugged your product or service and established sales, use resellers to accelerate, expand, or supplement your efforts. But do not think that resellers can establish your product or service for you or provide the quality feedback you'd get from selling to customers on your own.

POSITION AGAINST THE LEADER

Seth Godin, the author of *The Bootstrapper's Bible,* makes a strong case for positioning against the market leader or against accepted ways of doing things as a valuable bootstrapping technique. Rather than trying to establish your product or service from the ground up, you utilize the existing brand awareness of the competition.

Consider these examples of how you can do it:

- Lexus: "As good as a Mercedes or BMW, but 30 percent cheaper"
- Southwest Airlines: "As cheap as driving"

- 7UP: "The Uncola"
- Avis: "We try harder" (than Hertz)

Positioning against the leaders or standard ways of doing business can save lots of marketing, PR, promotion, and advertising dollars, so pick the "gold standard" in your industry and isolate an important point of differentiation in your own product, such as

- cost
- ease of use
- convenience
- industrial design
- reliability
- speed/performance
- range of selection
- customer service
- geographic location

By spending millions of dollars and years of effort to establish its brand, your competition has done you a terrific favor—all you have to do is positioned against it. There is a catch, though, because successful positioning against a leader requires three conditions:

- The leader is, and remains, worth positioning against. Imagine, for example, if you had positioned your company against Enron when Enron was the darling of Wall Street.

- The leader doesn't get its act together and erode your advantage— for example, if you position your computer as faster than IBM's and then IBM quickly responds with an announcement of a radically faster model.

- Your product or service surpasses the competition's in truthful, perceptible, and meaningful ways. If not, no one will care about your hype. Worse, you'll lose your credibility, and credibility is hard to regain.

Still, for the near term, this can be a useful technique to enable you to explain what you do on a low budget.

TAKE THE "RED PILL"

This is your last chance. After this, there is no turning back. You take the blue pill—the story ends, you wake up in your bed and believe whatever you want to believe. You take the red pill—you stay in Wonderland and I show you how deep the rabbit hole goes.
—*The Matrix*, 1999

In *The Matrix* Neo chooses the red pill, which brings him face to face with the harsh realities of the world. If he had taken the blue pill, he could have lived in the comfortable fantasy of the Matrix.

The leaders of new organizations face the same choice: reality or fantasy. The choice is as simple as Neo's. If you want to be a successful bootstrapper, you have to take the red pill and determine how deep the rabbit hole called your organization goes. If you are serious about staying in touch with reality, these are the ten most important questions you can ask:

1. When is your product or service going to be ready for market?
2. What are your true, fully loaded costs of operations?
3. When will you run out of money?
4. How much of your sales pipeline is going to convert?
5. How much of your account receivables is collectible?
6. What can your competition's product or service do that yours can't?
7. Who are your nonperforming employees?
8. Are you doing all you can to maximize shareholder value?
9. What is your organization doing to change the world and make meaning?
10. How good are you as the leader of the organization?

GET A MORPHEUS

Every drug, even truth, needs a delivery system. In *The Matrix,* it was Morpheus, the character played by Laurence Fishburne. Who is Morpheus in your organization?

If you don't have one, you need to get one. Typically, your Morpheus is a chief financial officer, chief operations officer, controller, or accountant.

- The adult doesn't need to be a grump, but simply someone knowledgeable about the real-world operation of an organization. The person's role isn't "naysayer" but "realist."

- As such, this person is the yin to the CEO's yang. The CEO decides "what," while this person decides "how" and "why not." Their relationship is not an opposition but a counterbalance.

- Morpheus should have at least ten years of operating experience. A background primarily as a consultant, auditor, banker, journalist, or analyst is a bad idea because it's easy to "advise" but hard "to do." The single best question to determine if a person's background is adequate is "Have you ever fired or laid off someone?" If the answer is no, keep looking.

In actuality, your Morpheus may not wind up being a single person. During different phases and for different tasks, the Morpheus role may shift around, with

- a research-and-design Morpheus to tell you that what you're creating is flawed
- an operations Morpheus to tell you that your systems can't handle the business
- a finance Morpheus to tell you that you're spending too much (or too little) money
- an ethics Morpheus to tell you that you're inculcating the wrong values

Each organization has a need for a different kind of Morpheus, but all organizations need at least one of them to deliver the red pill, when necessary.

UNDERSTAFF AND OUTSOURCE

There's an age-old question that all CEOs face: Which is worse—to leave money on the table because you can't handle all the business, or to lay people off because you overestimated revenues? The thought of leaving money on the table makes my ears ring, but laying off people is worse.

At its peak, the headcount of Garage was fifty-two people. After a series of layoffs, I reduced the head count to under ten people. Sure, almost everyone at the time thought that the technology market was going "to infinity and beyond" (as Buzz Lightyear would say), so we weren't alone in ramping up the staff.

I made a mistake, though; CEOs are paid to do the right thing, not the same thing as everyone else. Overstaffing causes a wicked web of problems. Dealing with it is not simply a matter of lowering head count, as you'll have to face the issues of

- excess space locked in a long-term lease
- excess furniture and computers
- trauma in the organization as people are let go
- trauma in the lives of the people who are let go
- trying to hire different kinds of people (for your new reality) in the midst of letting others go
- going through gyrations to convince the world that you're not imploding

There's a short-term solution to understaffing, and that's to outsource as many functions as you can. Don't outsource strategic functions such as research and development,* marketing, and sales. But there's

---

*I've heard the arguments about why companies should do their software programming in Russia and India. Maybe this is a good strategy when the programming is just spitting out lines of code, but when you're working on version 1.0 of a product, I disagree. Programming at this stage of a company is more art than contract labor. Leonardo da Vinci surely would not have outsourced the table in *The Last Supper* and focused on the humans— although having read *The Da Vinci Code*, I'm not sure what to believe about him anymore.

little reason to calculate payroll internally when organizations such as PayChex* and ADP can handle this for you.

Do as I say, not as I did. If you want to bootstrap your organization, then intentionally understaff. You may leave some sales on the table, and you may not achieve escape velocity as fast as you'd like. But it sure beats laying people off or running out of money.

BUILD A BOARD

Many entrepreneurs believe that a board of directors is appropriate only for organizations that have raised boatloads of money and are fairly far along. According to this theory, until then, these organizations should make do with no board or with a board of only the internal team members.

This reasoning is wrong on several counts. First, good guidance is always valuable. The need for it is not dependent on the stage of the organization or the amount of capital it has raised.

Second, money, or the amount of capital you've raised, is not the only factor that can attract high-quality board members. Other factors include the innovativeness of your product or service, the meaning you're going to make, and your personality.

Building a board of high-quality directors—just as assembling a great team—without funding is solid testimony to your product or service and your evangelism skills. Plus, a great board will help you get money as much as money will help you get a great board.

SWEAT THE BIG STUFF

Bootstrapping goes awry when entrepreneurs focus on saving pennies to the detriment of the Big Picture. The reason for starting an organization is not to build desks out of sawhorses and doors—nor is it to

---

*Plus, the Buffalo Sabres need all the help they can get.

make Herman Miller a bigger company. Here is a list of the usual big stuff and small stuff entrepreneurs must manage.

SMALL STUFF
- office space
- furniture
- computers
- office equipment
- office supplies
- business cards and letterhead

BIG STUFF
- developing your product or service
- selling your product or service
- collecting the money for your product or service

Whenever you can do so reasonably, do the small stuff cheap and don't waste money on the accoutrements. Rick Sklarin, a former Accenture consultant, puts it this way: "Make one trip to Costco and be done with it." Do sweat the big stuff, however—but there isn't that much big stuff.

EXERCISE

The next time there's something that you "can't live without," wait for a week and then see if you're still alive.

EXECUTE

A friend at Stanford University, ex–Sun Microsystems, George Grigoryev, pointed out to me that the real enemy of bootstrapping isn't spending—it's failing to execute. If bootstrapping is all it took to succeed, every organization in the world would be using sawhorses and wooden doors for desks. Just because you're cheap doesn't mean you're effective. For this reason, here are the recommendations that George and I came up with about the art of executing.

- **SET AND COMMUNICATE GOALS.** The simple act of setting goals and communicating them increases the likelihood that your organization will achieve them. It gets everyone on the same page and provides a day-to-day guide for what employees need to do. This applies to every task: finalizing specifications, building a prototype, signing up early customers, shipping, collecting, recruiting, finishing marketing materials . . . the list is endless.

- **MEASURE PROGRESS.** Goals only work if you measure progress. As the old saying goes, "What gets measured gets done." This also means you'd better pick the right goals, or the wrong things will get done. In a startup, you should measure and report results every thirty days. As your organization gets older and more deliberate, you can shift to a quarterly schedule.

- **ESTABLISH A SINGLE POINT OF ACCOUNTABILITY.** If it takes more than ten seconds to figure out who is responsible for achieving a goal, something is wrong. Good people accept accountability. Great people ask for it. For the good of your entire organization, establish it. A person who knows he is being measured and held accountable is highly motivated to succeed.

- **REWARD THE ACHIEVERS.** The people you reward in a startup are the ones who deliver. You can use options, money, public praise, days off, or free lunches—it doesn't matter. What does matter is that you recognize achievers—and only achievers, not the people who are along for the ride.

- **FOLLOW THROUGH UNTIL AN ISSUE IS DONE OR IRRELEVANT.** We all like to work on the newest, hottest stuff. It's human nature. Who wouldn't rather be involved with the next breakthrough product rather than fixing the current one? Don't stop when something simply gets boring. Fixing bugs may be boring to you, but it's not to the customer who recently bought your product.

- **HEED MORPHEUS.** Realism is the ally of execution, so pay attention to what your Morpheus says. Everyone in a given company is in denial about something. Some denial is good for an entrepreneur—for example, denying that the "experts" are right when they say you can't succeed. The critical issue is whether the denial is ultimately going to hurt the organization. Insist on realism, and your organization will bootstrap better.

- **ESTABLISH A CULTURE OF EXECUTION.** Execution is not a one-time event. Nor is it a process where you check off goals as if your sixth-grade teacher were looking over your shoulder. Rather, execution is a culture that produces a set of organizationwide habits. The only way to establish this culture is for the CEO to set the right example: answering inquiries, solving problems, and promoting people who deliver results. This sends an unmistakable message: Execution counts in this organization.

FAQ

Q. How do I know when bootstrapping has taken us as far as we can go?

A. This is a seemingly logical question, but it will seldom come up in a real-world situation. If you're bootstrapping merrily along, you'll eventually be able to fund new efforts. More likely, the question you'll face will be, "What would I do if I had more capital?"

Q. Will I forsake growth—and maybe even success—if I bootstrap too much?

A. I can't come up with a single example of an organization that bootstrapped too much. There's greater danger of blowing an opportunity because of too much money than because of too little. Negatively stated, think of venture capital as steroids: It might give you an immediate advantage, but it could kill you.

Q. If I can successfully bootstrap an organization, do I even have to look for outside capital? What's wrong with doing it the old-fashioned way?

A. Respectively, no and nothing. Outside capital isn't the only way—it's simply one way. The goal is to build something great, no matter how you raise capital.

Q. If we don't have several million dollars in venture capital funding, will we not be taken seriously?

A. Only by people who don't matter. If you do raise this kind of money, use it to add to your credibility, but don't believe that it will guarantee your success. If you don't raise this kind of money, don't sweat it. Just build a great business and don't look back.

Q. With your emphasis on execution, what do I do if someone doesn't execute? Should I simply fire the person?

A. It's not that simple. Find the real reason that a person failed to execute. There may be problems that were out of his control. Isolate those problems and fix what you can. A good rule of thumb is to give the person the same "due process" that you'd like your board of directors to give you. When due process is exhausted, make the cut, and make it quickly and decisively.

RECOMMENDED READING

Godin, Seth. *The Bootstrapper's Bible: How to Start and Build a Business with a Great Idea and (Almost) No Money.* Chicago: Upstart Publishing, 1998.

Hess, Kenneth L. *Bootstrapping: Lessons Learned Building a Successful Company from Scratch.* Carmel, CA: S-Curve Press, 2001.

CHAPTER 6

The Art of Recruiting

It is essential to employ, trust, and reward those whose perspective, ability, and judgment are radically different from yours. It is also rare, for it requires uncommon humility, tolerance, and wisdom.

—Dee W. Hock

GIST

There are few tasks that face an entrepreneur that are more enjoyable than recruiting employees to a hot startup. What could be better than finding people to help change the world? And there are few factors that are more critical to the success of a startup than good people.

Good recruiting starts at the top: CEOs must recruit the best people they can find. Next, good recruiting requires looking beyond superficialities such as race, creed, color, education, and work experience. Instead, you should focus on three factors:

1. Can the candidate do what you need?
2. Does the candidate believe in the meaning you're going to make?
3. Does the candidate have the strengths you need (as opposed to lacking the weaknesses you're trying to avoid)?

If candidates pass these tests, then go get them, but in a smart way—by using all your weapons, negotiating at the right moment, and double-checking your intuitions.

After they're on board, you should define a honeymoon period during which both parties can analyze whether things are working out. Finally, as a philosophical framework, make the effort to "recruit" your employees every day—to make sure they want to come back the next day.

HIRE "A" PLAYERS

I start with the premise that the function of leadership is to produce more leaders, not more followers.

—Ralph Nader

Steve Jobs has a saying that A players hire A players; B players hire C players; and C players hire D players. It doesn't take long to get to Z players. This trickle-down effect causes bozo explosions in companies.

If there is one thing a CEO must do, it's hire a management team that is better than he is. If there is one thing a management team must do, it's hire employees who are better than it is. For this to happen, the CEO (and management team) must possess two qualities. The first is the humility to admit that some people can perform a function better than they can. Second, after making this admission, they need the self-confidence to recruit these people.

Admittedly, urging managers to hire A players is hardly a revelation, and yet many organizations are filled with bozos. This happens because most people don't heed this principle and because it is so difficult to filter out bozos. I can't force you to take this advice, but I can provide five ways to avoid hiring the wrong people:

- **DON'T CONFUSE CORRELATION AND CAUSATION.** A candidate may have worked at an organization when it achieved success; this doesn't necessarily mean he contributed to the success. He could have just been along for the ride. The rising tide floats all boats.

To separate the eagles from the dodos, find out what specific projects the candidate managed and analyze his results. Also, try to find someone inside the company who worked with the person to see if the candidate caused or correlated.

- **DON'T CONFUSE BIG-ORGANIZATION SKILLS WITH NEW-ORGANIZATION SKILLS.** Success in a big organization doesn't guarantee success in a startup. The skills needed in each context are different. A vice president of Microsoft (with its established brand, infinite resources, and 100 percent market share) may not be the right person for a "two guys in a garage" operation.

BIG ORGANIZATION SKILLS	STARTUP SKILLS
Sucking up to the boss	Being the boss
Generating paper profits	Generating cash flow
Beating charges of monopoly	Establishing a beachhead
Evolving products and services	Creating products and services
Market research	Shipping
Squeezing the distribution channel	Establishing a distribution channel

- **DRAMATIZE YOUR EXPECTATIONS.** Make it crystal clear that working in a startup is different from what they might be used to in their previous organization: "Can you function without a secretary, fly coach, and stay in cheap motels?" You might scare off a few desirable candidates this way, but it's worth risking this to avoid ending up with people who cannot function in a startup atmosphere.

- **READ THE TEA LEAVES WHEN CHECKING REFERENCES.** Because the laws in the United States prevent providing job references that may damage a candidate's ability to get a job, whenever you don't get a reference that's superlative, you are in effect getting a negative one. If the reference sends you to the human resources department, then you know the candidate had problems. (See the end of this chapter for more on reference checking.)

- **TRUST THE RICHEST VEIN.** Your current employees are the richest resource for finding great people and for preventing a bozo explosion at your organization. If your employees aren't motivated to bring in good staff, who is? If there's a close call between two candidates, and one is known by an employee, you should usually take that one.

Many entrepreneurs don't realize this, but startups need three kinds of A players: first, *kamikazes* who are willing to work eighty hours a week to achieve success; second, implementers who come in behind the first group and turn its work into infrastructure; third, operators who are perfectly happy running the infrastructure.

Thus, good hires should not only be better than the CEO and management team, they should also be different from them. Startups need people with diverse skills that complement, not overlap, each other. For example, a geek CEO should hire someone who has sales skills—not another engineer to handle sales.

HIRE "INFECTED" PEOPLE

It's not enough that candidates are good and different; they must also believe that your organization can change the world. They must be infected with enthusiasm for what you do. Working in a startup isn't easy: Salaries aren't as high as elsewhere, benefits aren't as generous, and there's always the risk of running out of money. Therefore, belief in what you're doing is as important as competence and experience. It's often easier to teach an infected candidate how to do a job than to teach an agnostic (or atheist) how to believe.

I recommend taking a chance with any reasonably qualified candidate who already believes in your meaning. This means that the person is a user of your product or service. For that reason your customer base is the most fertile ground for recruiting. For example, someone who loved using a Macintosh made a good candidate for Apple.

If the candidate isn't coming to you as a proven believer, then use these techniques to determine if he "gets it."

- Ask the candidate to demonstrate your product or service. (Companies with crappy products, though, run the risk of losing candidates this way.) Someone who truly loves a product or service will be able to present it to its advantage.

- Measure the amount of time the candidate talks about compensation, benefits, and perks versus your product or service. This provides a good approximation of whether the candidate views the position as a way to make money or to make meaning.

- Analyze the candidate's questions: Are they built on a strong foundation of knowledge about your organization? Or, is the candidate trying to figure out the basics—what you do, who your customer is, and who your competition is?

IGNORE THE IRRELEVANT

There is a shortage of A players in this world. Therefore, it's stupid (not to mention illegal) to make recruiting decisions based on gender, race, religion, sexual orientation, or age. Why reduce the gene pool by taking a limited view?

Your goal, remember, is to make meaning and change the world. Many people put too much emphasis on the experience and backgrounds of candidates. To misquote George Orwell, ignoring is bliss.

It sometimes pays to ignore the lack of the perfect and relevant background, while at other times it pays to ignore the presence of the perfect and relevant background. Both can ultimately be irrelevant.

- **EXPERIENCE IN A BIG, SUCCESSFUL ORGANIZATION.** As we discussed earlier, a big-organization pedigree is not necessarily a reliable predictor of success in a startup environment. These pedigrees might be good for fundraising, but there's scant room for window dressing in a startup. The relevant question, again, is, "Did the candidate help create the success, or was he along for the ride?"

- **EXPERIENCE IN A FAILED ORGANIZATION.** This is the flip side of experience in a big, successful organization. Many factors could have caused the failure of an organization—perhaps the candidate was one of them. Or perhaps not. Failure, however, is usually a better teacher than success. The candidate to avoid, though, is one who has a consistent history of working for failures.

- **EDUCATIONAL BACKGROUND.** You want smart people, not necessarily "degreed" people. The two are not the same. Steve Jobs never finished Reed College. Steve Case, the founder of AOL, went to Punahou.* Half the engineers of the Macintosh Division of Apple didn't complete college. I dropped out of law school, and Stanford Business School rejected me.

- **EXPERIENCE IN THE SAME INDUSTRY.** Industry experience is a double-edged sword. On the one hand, understanding the industry lingo and possessing preexisting relationships are helpful. On the other hand, a candidate who is stuck in his way of thinking about an industry ("this is what computer interfaces have always looked like") can be a problem.

- **EXPERIENCE IN THE SAME FUNCTION.** Functional experience is also a double-edged sword. Apple once hired an executive from the tampon business because we thought we needed consumer marketing expertise to sell Macintoshes as a consumer good. However, his experience did not effectively transfer to the computer business. On the other hand, Ford Motor Company built the first assembly line for cars using the expertise of people from meatpacking houses, granaries, and breweries.†

There is one final characteristic that should often be ignored: functional weaknesses. You wouldn't say that one of Steve Jobs's strengths is compassion. Nor is Bill Gates's strength aesthetic design. Should you therefore not hire the next Steve Jobs or Bill Gates because of such weaknesses? There are two theories in hiring people:

*This is an inside joke for people from Hawaii. Suffice it to say that I went to Iolani.
†Andrew Hargadon, *How Breakthroughs Happen: The Surprising Truth About How Companies Innovate* (Boston: Harvard Business School Press, 2003), 42–43.

- Find the candidate who lacks major weaknesses (but doesn't have major strengths).
- Find the candidate who has major strengths (even though he has major weaknesses).

The first line of reasoning is flawed because everyone has major weaknesses—it's just a matter of finding out precisely what they are over time. Performing well in one area is tough enough; trying to find people who can do everything is Mission: Impossible.

The second line of reasoning is the way to go. A team of people with major and diverse strengths is what your organization needs in the early days when headcount is low, and there's no room for redundancy. High achievers tend to have major weaknesses. People without major weaknesses tend to be mediocre.

EXERCISE

Think back about your first few jobs. True or false?

___ I was perfectly qualified.
___ I am holding candidates up to standards higher than the person who hired me used.

USE ALL YOUR TOOLS

As I write this in 2004, it seems silly to worry about recruiting, since people are desperate to get jobs. However, in good times or bad, it is hard to hire the best people, so when you are pursuing them, you have to use all your tools.

Most people think their recruiting tools are limited to salary and equity plus fringe benefits such as insurance and medical care. But there are more incentives at your disposal:

- **YOUR VISION.** For many people, money isn't the most important reward of a job. They will work for less to do more by making meaning and changing the world.

- **YOUR TEAM.** Don't limit the candidate's interviews to his immediate supervisor and co-workers. If you've got a few superstars in other departments, add them to the seduction process.

- **YOUR BOARD OF DIRECTORS, ADVISORS, AND INVESTORS.** There's likewise something powerful about meeting with these folks. They are usually well known, highly respected, and rich. They can influence candidates to accept your position, so ask them to spend some time with your top candidates.

- **RÉSUMÉ-BUILDING POTENTIAL.** Let's face it: Few people work for one organization for their entire career. If you can get a few good years out of great people and help them build their résumés, do it. Plus, you never know, they may stick around longer than you anticipated.

Once you decide on a person, don't hold anything back and use all your tools to hire him.

SELL ALL THE DECISION MAKERS

Most people assume that the sole decision maker in a job search is the candidate. Slightly more enlightened people consider the spouse of the candidate, too. However, accepting a position, particularly in a startup organization, is usually even more complex than this.

The decision makers can also include such relations as the children, parents, and friends of the candidate. It's easy to imagine someone asking a parent if he should go to work for a startup and being told, "Don't. It's too risky. Get a job in a nice, safe company that will be around a long time—like Arthur Andersen or Enron."

Therefore, be sure to ask the candidate who all his important decision makers are, and then work with the candidate to answer their concerns, too. However, be aware that some candidates may fear this is a trick question—*If I admit that my parents are part of the process, they'll think I'm a wimp and won't hire me*—so do your best to assure them that the question is a serious one.

You're going to have to do your best to find out who all the decision makers are in order to ensure the best fit for both your organization and the candidate. After you learn who all the decision makers are, sell them, too.

WAIT TO COMPENSATE

Many companies make the mistake of preparing an offer letter too early in the hiring process. They use it as a "strawman"* to get compensation details on paper in order to show how interested they are and to reach closure quickly. This is a big mistake.

An offer letter should come at the end of the recruiting process. It is not a negotiating tool to get the candidate to say yes, but simply a way to confirm a verbal agreement. It's like a marriage proposal: Make it when you know the answer will be yes.

INTERPRET THE LIES

Amy Vernetti, a headhunter at Kindred Partners, came up with this list of the top ten lies of job candidates while she worked at Garage. Study them. They will help you avoid making hiring mistakes.

LIE	TRUTH
"I've got three other offers, so you'd better move quickly."	I've had three other interviews, and no one has flat-out rejected me yet.
"I was responsible for my company's strategic alliance with Microsoft."	I picked up the fax after Bill Gates signed the document.
"I'm leaving my current organization after only a few months because the organization isn't what the CEO told me it was."	I don't know how to do due diligence on an opportunity.

(continued)

*"A StrawMan has two features: it is easy to knock down, and it is a poor substitute for a real man" (http://c2.com/cgi/wiki?StrawMan).

LIE	TRUTH
"I've never been with a company for more than a year because I get bored easily."	It takes people about a year to figure out that I'm a bozo.
"I didn't really report to anyone at my old company."	No one wanted me in his department.
"Most of my references are personal friends because they know me best."	No one I worked for is willing to give me a reference.
"You've never heard of my last three employers because they were in stealth mode."	All the companies I worked for imploded.
"I'm no longer with the organization, but I maintain an excellent relationship with people there."	I was forced to sign a nondisparagement agreement to get my severance package.
"I am a vice president, but no one reports to me."	Any bozo can become a vice president at my company.
"I'm expecting to at least double my prior compensation package."	I was overpaid and understand that that I may have to take a cash hit for a good opportunity.

DOUBLE-CHECK YOUR INTUITION

According to common wisdom, to make great hires you must learn to trust your intuition about people. You'll frequently encounter two circumstances in recruiting:

- The candidate's education and background aren't quite right. For these reasons, others don't think you should hire him. Your rational side says, *Don't hire him. He doesn't have the right experience,* but your intuition says, *Grab him.*

- The candidate is perfect on paper (education, work experience, etc.), and the rest of your team thinks that you should grab him. Your intuition, however, tells you to pass.

These are both situations when you want to trust what your intuition is telling you. Unfortunately, your intuition is often wrong. Perhaps you liked a candidate, so you softened up on the interview questions and reference checking. Also, you may remember when your intuition proved right and conveniently have forgotten all the times it was wrong. Follow this procedure* to balance any undue influence from your intuition:

- **PREPARE A STRUCTURE FOR THE INTERVIEW BEFOREHAND.** You and your team should decide on exactly the attitude, knowledge, personality, and experience that are necessary for the position before you conduct interviews.

- **ASK QUESTIONS ABOUT SPECIFIC JOB SITUATIONS.** For example, ask the following kinds of questions for a vice president of marketing position:

    How did you manage a product introduction?

    How did you determine the feature set of a new product?

    How did you convince engineering to implement these features?

    How did you select your PR firm?

    How did you select your advertising firm?

    How did you handle a crisis such as a faulty product?

- **STICK TO THE SCRIPT.** Minimize spontaneous follow-up questions and making up new questions in real time. If you're afraid that you, and therefore your organization, will appear rigid and standoffish to the candidate, explain that you're using a technique from "this book about startups" that you read and that you're normally not like this.

- **DON'T OVERDO OPEN-ENDED, TOUCHY-FEELY QUESTIONS.** For example, any half-decent candidate can bluff through questions such as "Why do you want to work for this organization?" More pointed questions are better: "What are the accomplishments you're most proud of?" "What were your biggest failures?" "What was your most gratifying learning experience?"

*Inspired by David G. Meyers, *Intuition: Its Powers and Perils* (New Haven, CT: Yale University Press, 2002), 196.

- **TAKE COPIOUS NOTES.** You'll need these notes to accurately remember what each candidate said. Don't depend on your memory because it will be warped by the passing of time and your subjective reactions to candidates.

- **CHECK REFERENCES EARLY.** Many organizations check references for a candidate to whom they've already decided to make an offer. This is a setup for a self-fulfilling prophecy because you're going to hear, and want to hear, comments that affirm your decision.

  Big mistake. You should use reference-checking as a means to decide whether the candidate is even acceptable, and not as a confirmation of a choice that you've already made. (More on reference checking appears at the end of this chapter.)

After this process, if your intuition is telling you one thing and "the facts" are telling you another, answer these questions:

- Should you like the candidate (because he is well qualified), but you don't?
- Should you not like the candidate (because he is not well qualified), but you do?
- Is there a factual and objective basis for your intuition?
- Would the interview have gone differently if you had conducted it over the phone? Let's not deny that the physical appearance of a person can influence your decision.

After taking all these precautions, follow your intuition. Going with my intuition has served me well in the past (granted, my memory is selective). And I would be a hypocrite to tell you to rely on "just the facts" because Apple hired me—an ex–jewelry-schlepper with a psychology degree—to evangelize the most important product in the company's history.

On paper, I was not even close to being the right person for evangelizing Macintosh to software developers. Somebody's gut reacted positively—or at least not too negatively—to me. Either that or Steve Jobs was out of the office that day.

APPLY THE STANFORD SHOPPING CENTER TEST

There's one more test to apply to a candidate once you're past double-checking your intuition. It's called the Stanford Shopping Center Test. This mall is located in Palo Alto and is close to Menlo Park, Portola Valley, and Woodside—communities populated by entrepreneurs, venture capitalists, and investment bankers. Whenever you shop there, you're bound to see someone from the high-tech business.

A few years ago, I was at the mall when I caught sight of a Macintosh software developer, but he had not yet seen me. I instantly made an abrupt turn in order to avoid having to talk to him because he was a pain in the ass. This experience led me to conceive the Stanford Shopping Center Test.

This is how it works. Suppose you are at a shopping center. You see a candidate (or employee or partner or service provider) before he notices you. At that point, you can do one of three things:

1. Scoot over and say hello.
2. Figure that if you bump into him, fine. If not, that's OK, too.
3. Get in your car and go to another shopping center.

No matter what your intuition and a double-check of your intuition tell you, you should only hire and keep people that you'd hustle over to and engage in a conversation. If you find yourself picking option 2 or 3, don't make the hire. Life is too short to work with people you don't naturally like—especially in a young, small organization.

(By the way, if you pick option 2 or 3 for someone currently employed at your organization, either fix the situation or get rid of the person.)

DEFINE AN INITIAL REVIEW PERIOD

Despite your best efforts, your recruiting process (or your intuition) is sometimes wrong, and the new hire does not perform to your expectations. For me, one of the hardest tasks is to admit this mistake and correct it.

However, if there's one thing that's harder than firing someone you don't want around, it's laying off people you want to keep. Rest assured, if you don't make a course correction or terminate people who aren't working out, you increase the probability of having to lay off people who are.

To make this easier on both the organization and the employee (because it's also the right thing for the employee to stop working for the wrong organization), establish an initial review period with incremental milestones. The more concrete the performance objectives, the better. For example, objectives for a salesperson might include

- completion of product training
- completion of sales training
- participation in five sales calls

This period needs to be longer than the hiring afterglow, but shorter than the time it takes for the predominant feeling to become *Why did we hire this person?*

In short, ninety days.

Establish an understanding that after ninety days, there will be a joint review in which both sides discuss what's going right, what's going wrong, and how to improve performance. Some issues will be your fault!

DON'T ASSUME YOU'RE DONE

In 2000 Garage recruited a well-known investment banker from a big-name company. It took weeks of wooing and two rounds of offers and counteroffers as his current employer sweetened his current compensation.

Finally, we landed him. Everything was set to go. He and his family even came to our company BBQ. A few weeks later he started at our firm. He showed up for work for a few days. Then he called in sick for a couple of days. Late one night, I got an e-mail from him saying that he was resigning.

He left Garage to work for a former client of the investment bank. A few months after that, he returned to his original employer. I learned three lessons from this experience:

- We should have checked him out better; perhaps we would have learned that he wasn't suited to a startup.

- Beware of "big-company disease." That is, once someone works for the top-of-the-line, most lucrative, most prestigious firm, it's extremely unlikely that the person is right for a bootstrapping startup.

- Never assume you're done. Recruiting doesn't stop when a candidate accepts your offer, nor when he resigns from his current employer, nor on his last day at his current employer—not even after he starts at your organization.

In actuality, recruiting never stops. Every day is a new contract between a startup and an employee.

MINICHAPTER: THE ART OF REFERENCE CHECKING

You can't build a reputation on what you're going to do.
—Henry Ford

Reference checking is a crucial part of recruiting a great team. However, startups usually do it in a cursory and casual way—usually *after* the company has made a hiring decision. Courtesy of Amy Vernetti, the headhunter for Kindred Partners, here's a short course on reference checking to improve your results.

The goal of referencing is not to disqualify a candidate, but to look for consistency in how the candidate represented himself. You are also looking for clues about whether the candidate can be effective at your organization.

In order to paint a complete picture of a candidate, you should speak with at least two subordinates, two peers, two superiors, and two customers. Investors or board members are also interesting references.

These are suggested questions:

- How do you know this person? How long have you known him?
- What are your general impressions of him?
- How would you rank him against others in similar positions?
- What contributions has he made to the organization?
- How do others in the organization view him?
- What are his specific skills? What is he best/worst at?
- What are his communication and management styles?
- In what areas does he need improvement?
- Is he capable of functioning effectively in a small organization?
- How would you comment on his work ethic?
- Would you hire/work for/work with him again?
- Should I speak with anyone else about him?

In addition to following Amy's suggestions about reference checking, you should get unsolicited references from people the candidate did not provide, too. Find someone who knows someone at the company and check out the candidate. You can also cold call into the company and simply ask the operator to connect you to someone who worked with the candidate.

FAQ

Q. When interviewing candidates, should I be honest about our organization's weaknesses as well as our strengths?

A. Let me get this straight: You're wondering if you should lie to candidates knowing that if they take the job, they'll eventually discover that your organization sucks?

Always tell it like it is. Lower their expectations. You'll encounter three types of responses to your candor. Some candidates simply need an explanation of the problems. Go down the list of problems and explain them. Chances are, they just want to know what they're getting into, and you won't scare them off.

Other candidates want the challenge. For them, problems are opportunities. You should consider telling this type, "You're the guy we need to save us. Can you step up and be a hero?"

You will scare off the third kind of candidate. This person probably wasn't well suited to a startup anyway. You've done yourself a favor.

Q. Does it look bad to the outside world if we only have a few employees? Is it better to have six part-time employees rather than three full-time employees, for the sake of numbers?

A. Having six part-time employees for the sake of looking bigger is insane. If you're doing this for other reasons—offering flexible hours to get better people, for example—it's OK. But not for a silly reason like this.

Q. When is the right time to recruit CXO-level people: before or after funding the organization?

A. Many people think that the process of starting an organization is serial: A followed by B, followed by C, etc. It's not that simple. Starting an organization is a parallel process: You do A, B, and C at the same time. The answer to your question is that you're recruiting before, during, and after the funding process.

I caution you, however, against falling into this trap: An investor tells you that he would invest if you had a "world-class" CXO. You take this as a yes, recruit the person, and go back to the investor. Then the investor comes up with a different reason: "Good job. Now show us some customers actually paying for your product." The lesson is this: Don't recruit to make an investor happy. Recruit to build a great organization.

Q. Should I spend money on retainer-based searches or rely on my own capability to attract the best talent?

A. Prior to funding, your job is to use your passion to tap your network to find the right person without paying fees. After funding, use whatever you have to—including retainer-based searches.

Q. If asked, should I provide a salary range?

A. No. If you're asked directly, respond by saying something such as, "We will pay what it takes to get a great candidate." Then ask, "What is your current salary level?" This will teach them to ask tough questions.

The beginning of the interview process is too early to start mentioning numbers. Candidates will remember what you said—especially the top end of the range. And whatever number you throw out could affect the candidates' answers in the interviews.

Q. If my goal is to recruit "people more talented than myself," how do I retain control of the venture and avoid getting ousted from my own business?

A. This question says more about you than you probably intended. Your goal shouldn't be to "retain control" and "avoid getting ousted." Your goal should be to build a great organization. There may come a time when you should be ousted. Deal with it. Would you rather have an inferior organization that failed, but that you were in control of until the bitter end?

Q. I'm working with my best friend. Do I really need a legal agreement?

A. Yes, absolutely. Times change, people change, and organizations change. Difficult and inappropriate as it may seem, you must do this. Such a legal agreement may turn out to be the best thing for your friendship and your organization.

Q. What is a reasonable enticement and compensation for a member of my board of directors?

A. The range is usually .25 to .5 percent, but for an absolute superstar, I'd go as high as 1 to 2 percent of the company. If it takes more than this to get the candidate, move on. The person is more interested in making money than in making meaning.

Q. What do you do when you have to fire the partner who conceived the business, brought you in to help run it, trusts you, and is now clearly in over his head?

A. You take him aside and have a private conversation explaining the situation. You offer the person some choices about how to take a smaller role, but you are clear that such a move is necessary. A smaller role can mean taking a different position or serving only on the board of directors or board of advisors. Try to preserve the person's dignity. In most cases, there will be a blowup. Expect that. It might take years to heal your relationship, but that's how it goes.

RECOMMENDED READING

Lewis, Michael. *Moneyball: The Art of Winning an Unfair Game.* Waterville, ME: Thorndike Press, 2003.

Meyers, David G. *Intuition: Its Powers and Perils.* New Haven, CT: Yale University Press, 2002.

CHAPTER 7

The Art of Raising Capital

At a presentation I gave recently, the audience's questions were all along the same lines: "How do I get in touch with venture capitalists?" "What percentage of the equity do I have to give them?" No one asked me how to build a business!
—Arthur Rock

GIST

This chapter explains the process of raising capital from outside investors. These investors may be venture capitalists, management, foundations, government entities, or any of the three Fs: friends, fools, and family.

My experience is with the Silicon Valley venture capital industry, a group from which you may never try to get an investment. However, if you can raise capital from a Silicon Valley venture capitalist, you can raise capital from anyone. As the Frank Sinatra song goes, "If I can make it there, I'll make it anywhere."

Skillful pitching, which we covered earlier, is a necessary, but not sufficient, part of raising capital. More important are the realities of your organization: Are you building something meaningful, long-lasting, and valuable to society?

BUILD A BUSINESS

If there's someone to believe about raising money, it's Arthur Rock. He was a founder and chairman of Intel and backed companies such as Fairchild Semiconductor, Teledyne, and Apple. Many, many venture capitalists are simply lucky. To misquote Eugene Kleiner, a legendary venture capitalist from Kleiner Perkins Caufield & Byers, in a tornado even a dodo's investments can fly.

Arthur Rock is more than lucky, and the man is telling you this: If you want to get an investment, show that you will build a business. Make meaning. Make a difference. Don't do it for the money. Do it because you want to make the world a better place. This applies to the geekiest of technology startups as well as to low-tech, no-tech, and not-for-profit organizations.

If you do succeed in building a business, either investors will be fighting to give you money or you won't need their money. Both are good problems to have. On the other hand, if you perform unnatural acts to raise money, you probably won't build a business, and you probably won't get the money, anyway.

A logical and fair question is *How do I build a business without capital?* This was covered earlier, in Chapter 5, "The Art of Bootstrapping," but the bottom line is this: You find a way. As venture capitalist Hunt Green said, "Everything is always impossible before it works. That is what entrepreneurs are all about—doing what people have told them is impossible."

GET AN INTRO

Thank you for sending me a copy of your book. I'll waste no time reading it.

—Moses Hadas

In publishing, movies, music, and venture capital there's a fairy-tale scenario that goes like this: You submit a draft, script, song, or business plan to an organization. Despite the mounds of other submissions, the quality of your pitch is so stellar that someone frantically asks you to come in for a meeting. After one meeting, you cut a deal.

Dream on.

God as my witness, the following is a true story. A startup had given up on getting money from a top-tier venture capital firm because the startup sensed there was no interest. I asked a partner at the firm why it had passed, and he told me it was because his associate knew a company in Europe that was doing the same thing. Also, the company had supposedly achieved "100 percent market share in Europe and was coming to the U.S." Therefore, it was probably already too late for another entrant.

I asked the associate who the company was. He didn't know—a friend had told him about it. I contacted this friend, and he also didn't know who the company was. Apparently another friend had told him about the company, and about how it had 98 percent market share in a tiny vertical market in Eastern Europe (as opposed to all of Europe!).

Let's review: A friend told a friend who told an associate who told a partner not to bother looking at the company. This tale illustrates why you need an introduction by a credible third party to get a decision maker to take a serious look at your organization.

The point is not that the submission process should be a level playing field. The point is to tilt the playing field in your direction by getting an introduction by sources that investors respect:

- **CURRENT INVESTORS.** One of the most valuable services a current investor can provide is to help find additional investors. This is part of the game, so don't hesitate to ask for help. Most investors will at least listen to the recommendations of other, current investors.

- **LAWYERS AND ACCOUNTANTS.** When you pick a lawyer, an accountant, and a PR firm, look for connections as well as competence. Ask them if they will introduce you to sources of capital. Lots of firms can do the work, so find one that can both do the work and make introductions.

- **OTHER ENTREPRENEURS.** A call or an e-mail from an entrepreneur to his investors saying, "This is a hot company. You should talk to them," is powerful. Go to the investor's Web site to figure out which companies he's invested in—you may well know someone at one of them. If not, get to know someone—execs at these companies are probably easier to get to than the investor himself. For those who are starting not-for-profits, look at the organizations that the target foundations have funded.

- **PROFESSORS.** Investors are impressed by the suggestions of professors. In Silicon Valley, for example, a call or an e-mail from a Stanford engineering professor will get the attention of every venture capitalist around. I hope you did well in school!

What if you don't know these kinds of folks? It's a cruel world. Raising capital isn't an equal opportunity activity, so get out there and get connected. I've tried to help with a short course about schmoozing at the end of this chapter.

SHOW TRACTION

Generally, investors are looking for a proven team, proven technology, and proven sales. Investors rank these factors in different order, but the one factor that cuts through all the hyperbole is racking up sales. (In Silicon Valley we call this "traction"—in the sense that a tire grips the road and moves a vehicle forward.)

Traction counts the most because you've demonstrated that people are willing to open their wallets, take out money, and put it in your pocket. That's the bottom line. If you can do this, the provenness of your team and technology is less important. I don't know of an investor who would rather lose money on provenness than make money on unprovenness.

Traction takes different forms in different industries. It's a straightforward definition for companies with products or services: revenues. In other cases, revenue may not be the parameter:

Schools	Enrollment and student test scores
Churches	Attendance at services
Museums	Numbers of visitors
Volunteer organizations	Contributions and number of volunteer hours

This raises two logical questions:

- How can I show traction if I don't have any money to start the company?
- What if my product or service isn't finished yet?

The answer to the first question is a resounding "Who said it would be easy?" So review Chapter 5 ("The Art of Bootstrapping"), cut a consulting deal for a potential client, and do what you have to do.

The answer to the second question is more complex. There is a Hierarchy of Traction—with all due respect to Maslow's Hierarchy of Needs. This is the pecking order:

1. Sales (or the parameters discussed above for nonproduct or service companies)
2. Field testing and pilot sites
3. Agreement to field test, pilot, or use prior to shipment
4. Establishing a contact to pursue a field test

The higher you are in this hierarchy, the better. But if you don't at least have a contact for a field test, you will have a hard time raising money.

CLEAN UP YOUR ACT

Other than in times of irrational exuberance, most investors are looking for reasons not to do a deal. Statistically, they would be right because most deals don't pan out. Think of an investor's deal flow as a funnel. Two thousand business plans enter at the top of the funnel. Two hundred are moderately credible. One hundred are interesting enough to read. Forty undergo due diligence. Ten get funded. One makes a bundle of money.

Investors want to weed out the rejects as quickly as possible because they don't want to waste time, and obvious flaws make it easy to throw out a plan, so you must present a clean slate. Here are the areas in which flaws abound:

- **INTELLECTUAL PROPERTY:** Lawsuits, or the risk of lawsuits, by former employers claiming that your technology belongs to them; core technology belonging to a founder, not the company; infringement on someone else's patents.

- **CAPITAL STRUCTURE:** Ownership of the vast majority of the organization by a few founders who are not willing to spread it out; dominant control by an inflexible investor who doesn't want any dilution; substantially overpriced or underpriced previous rounds.

- **MANAGEMENT TEAM:** Married or related co-founders; unqualified friends or roommates in CXO-level positions; lack of relevant industry experience; criminal convictions.

- **STOCK OFFERINGS:** Grants of stock (as opposed to options) to consultants and vendors in lieu of payment; common stock sold to friends and relatives at high valuations; solicitation of investors who are not qualified according to securities laws.

- **REGULATORY COMPLIANCE:** Noncompliance with state or federal laws and regulations; nonpayment of payroll taxes.

DISCLOSE EVERYTHING

If there's crud that hasn't been—or cannot be—cleaned up immediately, then disclose it to investors. And do it early in the process. The later you reveal it, the harder it will get to do so and the more it will harm your credibility.

For example, Garage once invested in a company that disclosed that a potential investor had a consulting agreement with the company. This deal came to light shortly before the financing was closing. This investor was buying stock, as well as receiving stock and cash for consulting services. No other investor had a similar deal.

When the other investors found out about this arrangement, the deal almost collapsed. Had the company made a full disclosure earlier and explained why it made sense for everyone (which, in fact, it did), things would have gone much more smoothly. Unfortunately, a high-value investor bailed out because of this last-minute issue.

What if you started, or worked for, an organization that failed? There's no use in trying to hide this fact, because investors will uncover it. It's also poor form to blame anyone or anything else: the market, other employees, customers, or, in particular, the investors (no matter what the truth is).

My recommendation is that you do a *mea culpa*. That is, you accept as much blame for the failure as is justified and "confess" your sins. Sophisticated investors find this admirable, and many an investor has made boatloads of money betting on entrepreneurs who failed in earlier efforts. What's important is not that you failed—it's that you learned from your failures and are eager to try again.

The lesson is this: Clean up your problems or disclose your problems, but never hide your problems.

ACKNOWLEDGE, OR CREATE, AN ENEMY

Many entrepreneurs believe that investors want to hear that the organization has no competition. Unfortunately, sophisticated investors reach one or both of the following conclusions if entrepreneurs make such claims:

- There's no competition because there's no market. If there were a market, there would be others trying to win it.
- The founders are so clueless that they can't even use Google to figure out that ten other companies are doing the same thing.

Starting an organization to serve a market that doesn't exist or exhibiting cluelessness is not conducive to raising money. A moderate level of competition is a good thing because it validates the market. Furthermore, the fact that you are aware of your competition shows that you've done your homework.

It's your job to show how you are superior to the competition, not that it doesn't exist. A chart that explains what you and your competition can and cannot do is useful to accomplish this.

COMPANY	WE CAN DO, THEY CAN'T	WE CAN'T DO, THEY CAN
X		
Y		
Z		

You should list the things that you can't do and the competition can because this builds credibility, showing that

- You can realistically appraise competition.
- You can communicate your knowledge clearly and succinctly.
- You are willing to present facts that don't always make you look good.

You can also use this chart to promote the relevance of your product or service to the marketplace by mapping your capabilities to the needs of your customers. That is, the list of "what we can do" capabilities should immediately illustrate that there's a need for your product or service.

So be bold. Openly discuss your strengths and weaknesses. Doing so will make your strengths more believable.

Unfortunately, no one ever does it this way. Instead, they contrive a matrix that makes them look good—frequently with irrelevant, if not downright silly, parameters. Something like this:

	US	COMPANY X	COMPANY Y
Right-handed CEO	✓		✓
Drive hybrid cars	✓	✓	
Vegan employees	✓		
Use Open Source code	✓		✓

If you truly don't have competition, then zoom out until you can define some. Competition can be as simple as the reliance on the status quo, Microsoft (since at some point Microsoft will compete with everyone for everything), or researchers in universities. Pick something, because saying you have no competition at all is a nonstarter.

TELL NEW LIES

In a typical day, an investor meets with two or three companies and sees another four or five executive summaries. Each company claims to represent a unique and earth-shattering opportunity with a proven team, proven technology, and proven market. No company claims to be a bunch of losers who don't know what they're doing.

Also, while you might think that you and your meeting are the center of the universe, in fact you're just the 10:00 A.M. meeting, when there was already one at 9:00 A.M. and two more follow you at 1:00 P.M. and 3:00 P.M.

Part of the center-of-the-universe delusion is that entrepreneurs invariably believe that they're telling investors something new. For the sake of investors who are tired of hearing the same old lies and for the sake of entrepreneurs who hurt their case by telling them, here are the top ten lies that entrepreneurs tell investors. Study them carefully, and at the very least be prepared to tell new lies.

Lie #1: "Our projection is conservative."

Not only is your projection conservative, but you'll be doing $100 million by year 3. In fact, the company is going to be the fastest-growing company in the history of mankind. Your projection isn't conservative. Frankly, you have no clue what your sales will be.

I fantasize about the day an entrepreneur tells me, "Frankly, our projection is a number we're picking out of the air. We're trying to make them high enough to interest you, but low enough so that we don't look like idiots. We really will have no clue until we ship the product and see how it's accepted." At least that entrepreneur is honest.

Lie #2: "Gartner (Forester, Jupiter, or Yankee Group) says our market will be $50 billion in five years."

In Chapter 3 ("The Art of Pitching"), I discussed what listeners think when entrepreneurs try to "prove" market size, and I advocated "peeling away the onion" or catalyzing fantasy instead. To repeat my advice: Don't cite these numbers and expect to impress investors. No one comes in and says, "We're in a crappy little market." Everyone does what you do.

Lie #3: "Boeing is signing our contract next week."

As I said, traction is good. It really makes you fundable. But until a contract is signed, it's not signed. When the investor checks in a week, and the contract isn't signed, you've got a real problem. In five years, I've never seen a contract signed on time. Talk about Boeing and your big deals *after* they're done. In general, make sure that all surprises to investors are upside surprises.

Lie #4: "Key employees will join us as soon as we get funded."

Let me get this straight: You're two guys in a garage, you're trying to raise a few hundred thousand dollars, your product is twelve months from completion, and you're telling me that these well-known people are going to resign their $250,000 per year, plus bonus, plus stock option jobs to join your company?

When we've checked with these key employees about whether they're in fact all set to join the company, the response, more often than not, is, "I vaguely remember meeting the CEO at a cocktail party." If you're going to tell this lie, make sure that these potential employees are locked and loaded and ready to quit.

Lie #5: "Several investors are already in due diligence."

That is, "If you don't hurry, someone else will invest in us, and you won't have the chance." This works well in times of irrational exuberance, but it is generally a laughable tactic. The reality, and what the listener is thinking, is *You've pitched a few other investors, and they haven't gotten around to rejecting you yet.*

The odds are that the investors know one another better than you know them. They can easily call up their buddies and find out how interested another firm is in your deal. To pull this lie off, you'd better be either a great bluffer or smokin' hot, or you won't have a chance against the investor network.

Lie #6: "Procter & Gamble is too old, big, dumb, and slow to be a threat."

Procter & Gamble, Microsoft, Oracle, Ford . . . pick a successful company. Many entrepreneurs think that by making such a statement, they are (a) convincing the investor of their moxie, (b) proving that they can defeat an entrenched competitor, and (c) establishing a competitive advantage.

In reality, they are showing how naïve they are about what it takes to build a successful business. There's a reason why people such as Larry Ellison can keep the San Jose airport open late for their private jets while you and I are munching peanuts on Southwest Airlines. And it's not because they are old, big, dumb, and slow.

It's scary enough to investors that you are competing with an established company. Don't seal your coffin by showing how clueless you are by denigrating such competition. Instead, build the case for these kinds of alternatives:

- partnering with the competition
- flying under its radar
- addressing a niche that it can't or won't address

Lie #7: "Patents make our business defensible."

Patents do not make a business defensible. They might provide a temporary competitive advantage—particularly in material science, medical devices, and biotech companies—but that's about it.

Garage, for example, has a patent on the process of investors and entrepreneurs using the Internet to catalyze investments. Do I sleep better at night because of this? Has it prevented investment banks, laid-off investment bankers, and consultants from using the Internet to connect buyers and sellers of private placements? Would we try to enforce the patent? The answers are, respectively, no, no, and no.

By all means, file for patents if you can, but don't depend on them for much more than impressing your parents unless you have the time (years) and money (millions) to go to court. If Apple and the U.S. Department of Justice can't beat Microsoft in court, you can't, either.

When talking to investors, the optimal number of times to mention that your technology is patentable is one. Zero is bad because it implies you don't have anything proprietary. More than one mention means that you're inexperienced and think patents make your business defensible.

Lie #8: "All we have to do is get 1 percent of the market."

This is what venture capitalists call the Chinese Soda Lie. That is, "If just 1 percent of the people in China drink our soda, we will be more successful than any company in the history of mankind." There are four problems with this line of reasoning:

- It's not that easy to get 1 percent of the people in China to drink your soda.
- Very few entrepreneurs are truly going after a market as large as all the people in China.
- The company that came in before you said something similar about another market. So will the company after you.
- A company that is shooting for only 1 percent market share isn't interesting.*

The right thing to do, as I discussed earlier, is to either come up with a believable total addressable market figure or catalyze fantasy so the investor can come up with a number himself. But saying that all you have to do is get 1 percent of a big market labels you a bozo.

Lie #9: "We have first-mover advantage."

There are at least two problems with this lie. First, it may not actually be true. How can you possibly know that no one else is doing what you're doing? As a rule of thumb, if you're doing something good, five other organizations are doing the same thing. If you're doing something great, ten are. Second, first-mover advantage isn't all that it's cracked up to be. Being a "fast second" might be better—let someone else pioneer the concept, learn from their mistakes, and leapfrog them.

Lie #10: "We have a world-class, proven team."

The acceptable definition of *world-class* and *proven* in this context is that the founders created enormous wealth for investors in a previous company, or they held positions in highly respected, publicly traded companies. Riding the tornado of a successful company in a minor role, working for McKinsey as a consultant, or putting in a couple of years at Morgan Stanley doesn't count as a proven background.

---

*Every venture capitalist secretly wishes to fund a company whose greatest threat is an antitrust lawsuit by the U.S. Department of Justice and the European Union.

EXERCISE

Give the list of lies to a friend and ask him to listen to your pitch. How many of these lies do you tell? You fail the exercise if you tell more than two.

DON'T FALL FOR THE TRICK QUESTIONS

In addition to telling new lies, you also need to correctly answer trick questions. Investors pose these questions to see if you're inexperienced or dumb enough to utter the wrong answers. Use the following table as a guideline.

INVESTOR TRICK QUESTION	WHAT YOU WANT TO SAY	WHAT YOU SHOULD SAY
"What makes you think you're qualified to run this organization?"	"What makes you think you're qualified to run this venture capital firm?"	"I've done OK so far, getting us to this point. But if it ever becomes necessary, I'll step aside."
"Do you see yourself as the long-term CEO of the organization?"	"What did your limited partners see in you?"	"I've been focused on getting our stuff to market. I will do whatever is necessary to make this successful—including stepping aside if needed. Here are the logical milestones at which we can make this transition . . ."
"Is ownership control of the organization a big issue for you?"	"I'm going to be putting in eighty hours a week to make this successful, and you're asking me if I care how much of it I own?"	"No, it's not. I realize that to make this successful, we need great employees and great investors. They all need to have a significant stake. I will focus on making the pie bigger, not on getting or keeping a big part of the pie."

INVESTOR TRICK QUESTION	WHAT YOU WANT TO SAY	WHAT YOU SHOULD SAY
"What do you see as the liquidity path for the organization?"	"An IPO that sets a new record for valuation for NASDAQ."	"We know that we have a lot of hard work to do before we can even dream of liquidity. We're designing this company to be a large, successful, and independent entity. Right now, our heads are down, and we're working as hard as we can to to do this. An IPO would be a dream outcome—plus these five companies are possible acquirers in the future . . ."

Got this straight? Tell new lies and old truths—not vice versa!

HERD THE CATS

There may be fifty ways to leave your lover, but there are even more ways for investors to tell you no. Unfortunately, entrepreneurs can't take no for an answer (this is part of being an entrepreneur). Simultaneously, investors don't like to provide clear and unequivocal rejections; they prefer the SHITS technique: (Show High Interest, Then Stall). Here are the common responses (using the term loosely) that entrepreneurs receive:

- "You're too early for us. Show us some traction, and we'll invest."
- "You're too late for us. I wish you had come to us earlier."
- "If you get a lead investor, we'll be part of the syndicate."
- "We don't have expertise in your sector."
- "We have a conflict of interest with one of our existing companies." (Trust me, if they thought they could make money with your company, they'd resolve this conflict.)
- "I liked your deal, but my partners didn't."
- "You need to prove that your technology can scale."

Most of the time what the investor is really telling you is "When hell freezes over." But there are some cases in which investors are genuinely interested but not yet committed. You may get an investment from them, but it will be as hard as herding cats.

The key to herding the cats successfully is (to mix metaphors) to get one in the bag rather than several close to the finish line. It's helpful if this cat is a big, beautiful, and well-known one, but any cat that isn't your relative will do. Investors—like misery—love company.

Winning over an investor is not only about providing objective, quantifiable, and compelling information through your pitch, business plan, and references. It's as much a dating process as it is an analytic process. The investor who "might" have said no is still watching what you do:

- Did you try to establish contact after the pitch?
- Did you answer questions that came up in the pitch?
- Did you provide supplemental information that supports your case?
- Have you surprised the investor by closing big customers or meeting milestones early?
- Have other high-quality investors written you a check?

Persistence along these lines can pay off, and you can provide this sort of update weeks and months after your initial pitch to herd the cats. However, continuing to make contact without demonstrable, significant improvements in your story will change your status from "persistent" to "pest." And nobody funds a pest.

UNDERSTAND WHAT YOU'RE GETTING INTO

Raising money, particularly from venture capitalists, is a difficult and long process—and this is if it goes well. May the go-go days of the 1990s return, but they may not, and only a bozo would depend on timing the market.

To illustrate what kind of people professional investors and venture capitalists are, let me tell you a story. It's not an urban legend like the story about the guy who strapped a rocket engine on his car and plowed into the side of a mountain. I heard this story directly from the venture capitalist herself.

The woman in question took her father to dinner one night, to a swanky restaurant with valet service. On the way there, her father chided her for buying a snazzy BMW. She pulled up in front of the restaurant, and the two of them went in.

Several hours later, she and her dad emerged and saw that her car was still where she parked it. Seizing the moment, she told her father, "See? This is why I drive a BMW. Restaurants keep the nice cars out front. Now we don't have to wait for a valet to get it."

At that moment, an irritated valet approached her and said, "Lady, you took your keys with you. We couldn't move your car."

What can we learn from this slice-o'-life venture capitalist story?

1. Venture capitalists believe that the rules are different for them.
2. They believe they are entitled to special treatment.
3. You should leave your car running when you pull up to a valet service.
4. Venture capitalists aren't necessarily different from you and me—they just happen to manage hundreds of millions of dollars.

The correct answer is "all of the above." Allow me to demythify the aura of venture capitalists:

- They don't know any more than you do about your sector. Still, how could you not think that they do when they are managing hundreds of millions of dollars?

- Getting a top-tier investor doesn't guarantee that you'll succeed. These firms make many bets, and they assume that most won't pan out.

- The moment you take a dollar of outside money, you lose "control." Control has nothing to do with the math of voting shares. When you take outside money, you're obligated to all shareholders even if they own a minority position.

- Lower your expectations of what they can do for you, and you won't be as disappointed. Outside investors can open doors for you to kick-start sales and partnerships. They can help you find future investors. They can prevent you from making mistakes if they've seen other companies make similar mistakes. They can make the world take you slightly more seriously because "they invested in you." But this is about it.

FIND YOUR TRAIN TICKET

I cannot verify if this is a true story or an urban legend, but a good entrepreneur or writer never lets the truth get in the way of a good lesson.

Albert Einstein was on a train. He couldn't find his ticket after searching through all his pockets and bags. The conductor approached him and said something to the effect of, "Dr. Einstein, everyone knows who you are. We know that Princeton can afford to buy you another train ticket."

To which Einstein replied with something along the lines of, "I'm not worried about the money. I need to find the ticket to figure out where I'm going."

Like Einstein, you should worry not about the money, but about where you are going. If you figure out where you're going, the money will come.

MINICHAPTER: THE ART OF RAISING ANGEL CAPITAL

I shot an arrow into the air, and it stuck.

—graffito in Los Angeles

Professional investors and venture capitalists are not the only source of money for startups. There are also thousands of wealthy individuals who can provide funding. Raising money from these folks requires a different approach because their goals are different from those of professional investors. This doesn't mean they are easier to get money from—only different. This minichapter explains the process.

- **DON'T UNDERESTIMATE THEM.** They may care less about financial returns than professional investors, but this doesn't mean they are suckers. Approach them with the same level of professionalism as if you were pitching a top-tier venture capitalist such as Kleiner Perkins Caufield & Byers or Sequoia Capital.

- **UNDERSTAND THEIR MOTIVATION.** Where professional investors want to make money and maybe pay back society, many angels want to pay back society and maybe make money. Angels see two ways to pay back society: help young(er) people get a start, and help a product or service that makes meaning get to market.

- **ENABLE THEM TO LIVE VICARIOUSLY.** A side benefit that many angels seek is a chance to relive their youth or a romantic past. Even though they can't or don't want to start another entity, they can enjoy watching you do it.

- **MAKE YOUR STORY COMPREHENSIBLE TO A SPOUSE.** The "investment committee" of an angel is his or her spouse. It's not a bunch of geeks, pundits, or former entrepreneurs. This underscores the importance of making your business understandable in plain terms.

- **BE A NICE PERSON.** Whereas a professional might invest in a jerk because "money is money," an angel won't. Angels fall in love with entrepreneurs in a fatherly or motherly way: "She's a nice kid. I want to give her a start." So be nice, malleable, and approachable. Come to think of it, this attitude can't hurt when dealing with professional investors, too.

- **SIGN UP PEOPLE THEY KNOW OR HAVE HEARD OF.** Angel investing is often about socializing as much as profiting. Thus, if you can attract one member of the "club," you can usually get more to follow.

MINICHAPTER: THE ART OF MANAGING A BOARD

Being in the army is like being in the Boy Scouts, except that the Boy Scouts have adult supervision.

—Blake Clark

With money comes responsibility. One of the blessings and burdens of taking outside investments is that you will have to create a board of directors. This minichapter explains the art of board management.

The first issue is the composition of the board. Your major investors will require a board seat, so some choices are already made for you. In total, you need people with two kinds of expertise: company-building and deep market knowledge. Here are the typical roles that need to be filled:

- **"THE CUSTOMER."** This person understands the needs of your customers. He doesn't have to be a customer, but should be thoroughly versed in what your market wants to buy.

- **"THE GEEK."** This person provides a reality check on your development efforts. For example, is your technology defying the laws of physics? Even if you don't have a tech company, the question remains the same: Is your task possible?

- **"DAD."** Dad (or Mom) is the calming influence on the board. He brings a wealth of experience and maturity to help mediate issues and reach closure on problems.

- **"THE TIGHT-ASS."** This is the bad guy who tells you that you're full of sushi when you're lying. This person also pushes for totally legal and ethical practices.

- **"JERRY MAGUIRE."** This is "Mr. Connections." His most important asset is his Rolodex of industry contacts and his willingness to let your organization use it.

The second issue is creating a good working relationship with your board members. Here are some tips:

- **SAVE TREES.** Less paper is better than more paper. It is a mistake to bury your board in documentation because these are busy folks. Make your accounting and financial reports about five pages long. They should include a profit-and-loss statement, cash flow projections, your balance sheet, and a list of accomplishments and problems.

- **PROVIDE USEFUL METRICS.** On their own, accounting and financial reports aren't sufficient. Nonfinancial metrics—such as the number of customers, number of installations, or number of visitors to your site—are equally important. This information should add no more than three to four pages to your reports.

- **SEND THESE REPORTS TWO DAYS BEFORE A BOARD MEETING.** Board meetings are the time and place for discussing strategic issues—not for conveying the factual information contained in your reports. You should spend little time in the meeting communicating the facts—and a lot of time figuring out how to improve them in the future. Thus, it's useful to send your reports in advance. However, don't assume that your directors will read them—you still need to review them in the meeting.

- **NEVER SURPRISE A BOARD (EXCEPT WITH GOOD NEWS).** The worst time and place to announce bad news is at a board meeting—unless you want a pack of hyenas tearing your flesh from your bones. When you have bad news, meet privately with each member in advance and explain what happened.

- **GET FEEDBACK IN ADVANCE.** The corollary of never surprising a board is to prepare board members well in advance of key decisions. If you know that you are going to discuss a key issue at an upcoming meeting, then talk to each member before the meeting. They might provide feedback that will change your perspective about the decision.

FAQ

This FAQ is the longest in this book. Its length reflects how difficult the process of raising money is for most people. I answered the most common questions about this topic within the main body of the chapter, and I've included only the most specialized ones here.

Q. I've got a venture capitalist who wants to invest $5 million in my company! What should I expect in terms of how he will want to interact with the company?

A. As long as things are going well, a venture capitalist will leave you alone. Understand a venture capitalist's life: He's on as many as ten boards that meet at least quarterly and sometimes monthly; he has to raise money to invest and keep about twenty-five investors informed and happy; he's looking at several deals a day; and he's dealing with five other partners. He doesn't have the time to micromanage you—and if he thought he'd have to, he probably wouldn't have invested in you in the first place.

The more important question is "What can I expect from a good venture capitalist?" Here is the answer: five hours a month of mind-share during which he opens doors for you with prospective customers and partners and interviews candidates for high-level positions at your company.

Q. How can I identify the venture capital firms that have new funds with a maturity sufficiently far out so they align with my liquidity timeframe?

A. You're thinking too much. The timing of a fund is hardly ever a factor. Besides, the firm is going to pick you and not vice versa, and there is no way to predict a liquidity timeframe.

Q. What is the order of approaching the tiers of venture capitalists: tier one, then two, then three, or the other way around?

A. You're thinking way too much, too. Pitch almost any firm you can get into. After trying to raise money for nine months, you'll realize that all money is green. Plus, it's not at all obvious who is a tier-one, -two, or -three firm.

Q. What is the internal rate of return expected from tier-one, -two, or -three venture capitalists? How firm do they stand by that projection?

A. First of all, it is unlikely that a venture investor will admit that his firm is not a tier-one firm. Even if he did, he isn't saying to his partners and investors, "Since we're not a tier-one firm, let's just try to get 10 percent."

All venture investors are looking for a high return on your specific investment, not a return that matches their target average. (Remember: They know there is a high likelihood that your company will flame out.) But your question misses on another point. Although venture firms are ranked against one another by their IRR performance, venture investors do not evaluate individual deals by calculating prospective IRRs. Not even VCs are so arrogant to believe they are that visionary.

Practically speaking, investors look at cash-on-cash returns—that is, if I put in $1 million today, what can I reasonably expect to get back in four or five years? ($5 million would be a 5× return.) Expectations for cash-on-cash returns vary by the type of investor and the sector of investment, not by the prestige of the firm. For an early-stage, high-tech investment, you had better be able to convince the investor that there is a realistic plan for returning 5× to 10× his money in three to five years.

Q. **Should I admit that our sales to date are lackluster (or even nonexistent)?**

A. Yes, but I would spin it: Your sales aren't lackluster—you're simply "early in the sales cycle with an extremely innovative product." Also, this is why the longer you can bootstrap and get to revenue, the better.

Q. **Should I admit to the venture capitalist that I am new to all of this?**

A. You won't have to because it will be obvious. Thus, you might as well tell the truth. However, to ameliorate this situation, surround yourself with directors and advisors who are experienced. Also, express clearly that you'll "do what's right for the organization and step aside if this is the right thing to do."

Q. **How much do venture capitalists talk among themselves? Will my faux pas in front of one be the talk of the watering hole and poison the well for me with the others?**

A. It's unlikely that venture capitalists will talk about you because there isn't enough time in the day to discuss all the lousy meetings and clueless entrepreneurs. You'd have to do something astoundingly stupid to be a topic of conversation.

Q. **Is it necessary to have hired a law firm and accounting firm prior to fundraising?**

A. It's not necessary, but it's better if you have a law firm for two reasons.

First, assuming you pick a law firm that's recognized for its corporate finance/venture capital work, it shows that you know what you're doing. Second, you need an experienced corporate finance lawyer to work through the paperwork of a financing. An accounting firm is less important because there's probably not much to account for yet.

Q. Is it better to ask for the cash to support the whole project up to a liquidity event or just what is needed for the first one or two years?

A. You can't possibly know if there will be a liquidity event, when it will occur, and how much money you'll need to get there. However, what you want to get, and what investors want to give, is enough capital to get to the next big milestone, plus six months of cushion for when you're late.

Q. Does my business need to be fully functioning and profitable in order to attract investment capital?

A. The venture capital business is cyclic—some would say bulimic. During times of feast, venture capitalists will fund anyone who can boot PowerPoint. During times of purging, most venture capitalists turn cautious and want "fully functioning and profitable" companies.

Your job is to find venture capitalists who make early bets on "unproven" companies. When venture capitalists tell you that they only invest in "proven" companies, they're lying. What they are saying is, "We don't get it, so we're blowing you off by telling you this. If we really got it and believed, we'd take the chance with you."

Q. Does the existence of a clear leader in my target market preclude me from getting funding?

A. I can unequivocally say, "It depends." If it's early in the life cycle of the market, and it's "clear" that the market will be huge, you can get funding. Commodore was the clear leader in personal computers, and plenty of companies got funded after it. On the other hand, it would be difficult in a mature, capital-intensive industry such as automobiles.

It also depends on the investor. Some will be scared off by a market leader. Others will see the existence of a market leader as proof that there is a market and be willing to take the leader on.

There's one more thing to think about. Your question is specifically about funding. However, fundability and viability are not the same thing. Your idea to take on the market leader may not be fundable, but it could still be viable, so don't let negative responses from investors stop you.

Q. **Is it better to have fewer, bigger investors or numerous, smaller investments?**

A. You should be so lucky to have the choice. Fewer investors means that there are fewer relationships to manage. Also, if bringing in more investors means you're also getting less sophisticated ones, forget it.

However, there are several compelling reasons to get additional investors: (1) More investors means that there are more people helping you by opening doors, recruiting, and generating buzz. (2) When you need additional capital, it's nice to have several sources already in the deal. (3) It's dangerous to have only one investor calling the shots in case you have a disagreement.

Q. **When accepting angel money, is it reasonable and customary to have a buy-out clause, to allow me to retain my stock if I am able to pay back the angel's loan with interest?**

A. Absolutely not. Angels are putting money into your company at the riskiest time, so they should benefit as much as anyone. If you do pull off a buy-out clause, you'll rack up bad karma points—and a startup needs all the good karma it can get.

Q. **Should current investors attend company pitches to prospective investors?**

A. If it's OK with the prospective investor, this is usually positively viewed: "The current investors care enough to come with the company to our meeting." If the current investor is a famous person, by all means bring him or her.

Q. **Which would appeal more to investors: a product concept that has a proven billion-dollar market in which there are already some big players, or a product idea that will create a new, potentially billion-dollar market that has no competitors in the short run?**

A. This depends on the investor. There are a handful of investors who like "brave new world" investment, but the vast majority are similar to buffalo: running with their heads down toward a cliff because the rest of the herd is, too. At some level, raising money is a numbers game: You've got to make a lot of pitches to find one investor to write a check.

Q. **Which should we have more focus on: pitch how the product solves pain and competitive analysis, or pitch how the investors can get *x* percent return?**

A. The former, never the latter. No one can predict when and how liquidity will occur. Attempting to do so will make you look silly.

Q. **When should an entrepreneur give up on getting capital from an investor?**

A. I've never seen an entrepreneur reverse a negative decision by arguing. When an investor says no (in so many words, as discussed earlier), accept the decision gracefully.

Do go back, however, when you can produce "proof." You get proof by finishing your product or service, opening prestigious accounts, raising money from other sources, and building a great team. Persistence, with proof, works.

Q. **What is a reasonable salary that a CEO should set himself up with that will not scare an investor away?**

A. This is hard to answer in absolute numbers. Circa 2004, for technology startups, the answer is probably $125,000 per year. An answer that can better stand the test of time is this: The CEO should not be paid more than four times the lowest-paid full-time employee.

Q. **Angels want entrepreneurs to have some skin in the game. I don't have any money to invest in the business. How do I overcome this? What do venture capitalists look for these days as far as "skin in the game"?**

A. An entrepreneur's skin in the game, for a venture capitalist or an angel, is nice to have—not a necessity. Certainly you shouldn't believe that because you were stupid enough to put money into a lousy idea, other investors will follow suit.

If you think that the only reason a potential investor declined was because you didn't have skin in the game, you were going to get a negative answer anyway. What's more important is how long you've been working on the product and bootstrapping the company and what progress you've made.

Conversely, if the investor agrees to provide capital primarily because you have skin in the game, then the investor is a fool, and you wouldn't want him. Also, in almost all cases, you will have a lot of skin in the game in the form of days of sweat equity.

Q. **If an angel investor asks what his return will be, what is the best answer?**

A. The best answer is to tell him that he must not be a sophisticated investor because such an investor would know better than to ask a question that has no answer. I'll bet, however, that you don't have the guts to do this. Instead, you can ask him to go over your financial projection with you and then ask him, "What do you think is realistic?"

Q. **What do I wear to meetings with venture capitalists?**

A. It depends on what part of the country you're in. On the East Coast, you should wear a jacket and tie. On the West Coast, you can be much more casual—Dockers and a polo shirt will do. No matter where you are, if you're the geek genius, you can probably get away with a clean T-shirt and jeans.

Q. **If I do not have an IPO or acquisition as my exit strategy, will I ever be able to attract investors? Would investors ever be interested in making their return through profit sharing or a buy-out from the founders of the company in five to ten years?**

A. Only if the investor is your mother. If the investors are professional investors, you can forget about raising money without a shot at an IPO or acquisition. If they're angels, investing in your organization might represent a flight of fancy or sympathy—then liquidity doesn't matter as much. But profit sharing or buying out investors is attractive to few investors.

Q. **Do entrepreneurs have to accept the valuation proposed by the venture capitalist who wants to invest into their business?**

A. Whatever the first offer, ask for a 25 percent higher valuation because you're expected to push back—in fact, if you don't push back, you may scare the venture capitalist if he thinks you're not a good negotiator. It would be nice to have some arguments to show why you believe your valuation should be higher—saying that this book told you to push back isn't sufficient.

At the end of the day, though, if the valuation is reasonable, take the money and get going. You'll see that either you will make more money than you ever thought possible or your organization will die. In either case, valuation and owning a few more percentage points seldom make a difference.

For a rough approximation of your valuation, circa 2004, you can also use Kawasaki's Law of Premoney Valuation: For every full-time engineer, add $500,000. For every full-time MBA, subtract $250,000.

If this is too unscientific for you, then use services such as VentureOne (www.ventureone.com) or VentureWire (www.venturewire.com) for information about current financings.

Q. **How can one protect an idea, given that few investors will sign an NDA (nondisclosure agreement)?**

A. You're right. Few investors will sign one, and even if they did, simply hearing your idea had better not make it copyable. I've never seen a case where an entrepreneur told an investor about an idea, and the investor ripped it off.

Investors are looking for people who can implement ideas, not simply come up with them. Ideas are easy. Implementation is hard—and where the money is. Quite frankly, few investors are capable of implementing an idea—that's why they're investors . . . but I digress.

Here are the fine points of using an NDA:

- Never ask an investor to sign one to have a first meeting or in the first meeting. No one who would sign one this early is an investor you'd want.

- If you're asking for an NDA to merely discuss your idea, keep your day job, because you're clueless. To this day, I get asked to sign an NDA to hear such ideas as selling books online!

- Freely circulate your executive summary and PowerPoint pitch. These documents should entice investors to go to the next step. They should not reveal your magic sauce.

- Ask for an NDA if an investor is interested in your deal and wants to learn more at the bits-and-bytes or molecular level. It is reasonable for an interested investor to ask this in the due diligence stage. This is most relevant for life sciences and material sciences companies.

- Once patents are filed, you should feel pretty safe in discussing your magic sauce under an NDA—not that you'll have the time or resources to sue for patent infringement.

The bottom line is still that the best protection of an idea is great implementation of the idea.

Q. When do I stop trying to find/negotiate a better deal and take what's offered?

A. It's a good idea to stop looking and negotiating if you can't meet payroll. If the deal that you're offered is within 20 percent of what you wanted, take it. Focus on building your business, not finding the best deal. In the long run, the quality of your business determines how much money you'll make, not the deal you cut years before with an investor.

Q. Should I worry more about dilution, the real needs of my business, or the amount the investor wants to put in?

A. Here's the priority: the real needs of your business, the amount the investor wants to put in, and, last and least, dilution.

Q. How do I get more value out of my board of directors?

A. The first and most important step is to take away their Blackberrys during board meetings. Then, generally, you ask. Surprisingly, many entrepreneurs are too intimidated by their board to actively manage them. Give them assignments and hold them accountable. They're holding you accountable, too.

RECOMMENDED READING

Stross, Randall E. *eBoys: The True Story of Six Tall Men Who Backed eBay, Webvan, and Other Billion-Dollar Startups*. New York: Crown Business, 2000.

Proliferation

CHAPTER 8

The Art of Partnering

Alliance, n. *In international politics, the union of two thieves who have their hands so deeply in each other's pockets that they cannot separately plunder a third.*

—Ambrose Bierce

GIST

Anyone who took part in the dotcom phenomenon of the 1990s developed a lot of partnerships. There were research partnerships, marketing partnerships, distribution partnerships, and sales partnerships. Frankly, there were more partnerships than there were revenues.

What most organizations learned is that partnerships are hard to make work. Though both parties wanted 2 + 2 to equal 5, they ended up with 3 instead. The problem is that glamour, flattery, and potential press coverage often seduced organizations into entering nonsensical collaborations.

The gist of good partnering is that it should accelerate cash flow, increase revenue, and reduce costs. Partnerships built on solid business principles like these have a much greater likelihood of succeeding.

Once you understand this, a partnership is simply a matter of implementation: making sure the people who do the real work buy into it, finding internal champions, focusing on strengths, cutting win–win deals, waiting for the right moment to bring in lawyers and legal documents, and establishing ways to end the relationship.

PARTNER FOR "SPREADSHEET" REASONS

An effective partnership can produce attractive results for a startup. It can speed entry into a new geographic area or market segment, open additional channels of distribution, accelerate new product development, and reduce costs.

I call these "spreadsheet" reasons because they change your financial forecast. Unfortunately, many organizations form partnerships for reasons that don't affect spreadsheets. Instead, they enter into them for a halo effect, to silence critics, because everyone else is doing them, or for the thrill of the chase.

For example, Apple and Digital Equipment Corporation formed a partnership in the late eighties in response to criticism of both organizations by the press. In short, Apple did not have a data communications story, and Digital did not have a personal computer story.

Little came of this alliance—certainly no products that vaulted Apple into big-business legitimacy or DEC into personal computer coolness. I doubt that spreadsheets at either company were affected, unless it was to reflect increased costs. It was, at best, a PR ploy to get the press off the backs of both organizations.

At least I learned a valuable lesson from that experience: Never form a partnership to make the press happy.

Apple created a much more successful partnership with a startup called Aldus Corporation, the publisher of PageMaker. At the time, Apple was floundering because big businesses perceived Macintosh as a cute little graphics toy, not a "business computer."

Apple needed a "killer application" that would jumpstart the sale of Macintoshes. Simultaneously, Aldus needed help selling its software by getting inventory into the distribution channel, educating retail salespeople, opening major accounts, and training end users.

This was perfect serendipity: Each organization needed the other to increase revenue. With its sales force, advertising, and marketing clout, Apple could help Aldus achieve critical mass. Aldus did its part by providing a compelling reason for people to buy Macintoshes instead of Windows computers.

The Apple–Aldus partnership created a new market called desktop publishing, and desktop publishing "saved" Apple and "made" Aldus. As they say, the rest is history.

EXERCISE

Go back to the bottom-up revenue forecast that you made in Chapter 5, "The Art of Bootstrapping." Does the partnership you're thinking about cause you to change any numbers?

DEFINE DELIVERABLES AND OBJECTIVES

If you accept the theory that the foundation of a good partnership is spreadsheet reasons, you'll understand why the next step is to define deliverables and objectives such as

- additional revenues
- reduced costs
- new products and services
- new customers
- new geographic markets
- new support programs
- training and marketing programs

There are two reasons why very few companies ever define deliverables and objectives. First, the partnership is built on sand, so it's difficult even to come up with deliverables and objectives. This is a bad omen.

Second, and less depressing, is that people don't have the discipline to establish these deliverables and objectives because they are too busy, disorganized, or lazy—or they are simply afraid of measuring results.

Here is a checklist of areas that should be covered:

- What will each organization deliver?
- When will they deliver it?
- Where will they deliver it?
- What interim milestones must each organization meet?

You'll find that by basing a partnership on spreadsheet numbers and defining deliverables and objectives, you've tripled the probability of the partnership's succeeding.

ENSURE THAT THE MIDDLES AND BOTTOMS LIKE THE DEAL

A second fundamental flaw of the Apple–Digital partnership was that the middles and bottoms (that is, where the real work is done) of both organizations didn't believe in it.

As an Apple employee at the time, I remember thinking, *What would a bunch of East Coast, minicomputer people add to Apple's story?* It's safe to assume that the DEC employees were thinking, *Why are we partnering with a flaky California company made up of hippies wearing Birkenstocks and Grateful Dead T-shirts who sit around in beanbag chairs all day?*

If you want to make a partnership work, don't focus on getting CEOs and upper management to agree and show up at the press conference. Ensure, instead, that the middles and bottoms understand the partnership, want to make it work, and value each other's contributions.

This cooperation starts when there is a true win–win solution, and both sides need each other. An announcement, if any, should come *after* the partnership is working well. Indeed, the best partnerships form when the upper management of each company is barely involved.

FIND INTERNAL CHAMPIONS

To form a successful partnership, both organizations need an internal champion to keep the partnership going. CEOs are seldom effective in this role because most CEOs have attention-deficit disorder. It's got to be a person or a small group who truly believes in the relationship and will live or die by it.

Many people have heard of John Sculley, the former CEO of Apple. Fewer people have heard of John Scull. John Scull was the desktop publishing champion inside Apple. The year was 1985, and John was the point person for Apple's efforts in this nascent market.

At any given point, he worked with Apple departments such as engineering, sales, training, marketing, and PR to help Aldus. Simultaneously, he worked with Aldus to fill Apple's needs for product information, copies of the software, and analysis of the needs of corporate customers. Additionally, he proselytized desktop publishing to journalists and pundits. To both internal employees and external parties, John was clearly established as Mr. Desktop Publishing.

If desktop publishing had failed, it would have been John's fault. Since it succeeded, it was many people's idea. (Such is the nature of a champion's life.) And arguably, if it had failed, there would be no Apple today. Here are the key takeaways from John's success with desktop publishing:

- **IDENTIFY A SINGLE POINT PERSON IN EACH ORGANIZATION.** The partnership's success can't be built on a matrix where multiple organizations each contribute a slice of their time.

- **MAKE SUCCESS OF THE PARTNERSHIP THE SOLE GOAL OF THE CHAMPION.** For the point person, nothing but the partnership counts. Thus, the champion can seldom be an executive because executives always have something else to do.

- **EMPOWER THE CHAMPION.** Making a partnership work involves cutting across internal departments, priorities, and turfs. It can require stepping on people's toes and getting them to do things they don't want to do. For all these reasons, the champion must be empowered, and people have to know he's empowered. It's also helpful, as in the case of John Scull, to have a name that sounds similar to the CEO of the company.

ACCENTUATE STRENGTHS, DON'T COVER WEAKNESSES

The third fundamental flaw in the Apple–DEC alliance was that it was built on weakness. Both organizations were trying to ameliorate fundamental gaps in their product offerings. The philosophy was "You cover up our weakness, and we'll cover up yours. Together, we'll fool everyone."

A far better philosophy is to accentuate the strengths of both partners: "You do this really well; let us help you do it even better. We do this really well, please help us do it even better."

In the Apple–DEC example, it would have gone this way: "Apple, you build a great personal computer. If it could do data communications better, it would be even better." And, "DEC, you really understand data communications. If you could bring data communications to the masses because of ease of use, it would be even better."

By contrast, the Apple–Aldus partnership did accentuate each party's strengths. Apple's strengths were its marketing resources, field sales force, trainers, and national account connections. Aldus's strength was its knowledge of page composition software and publishing.

CUT WIN–WIN DEALS

To make the flow of products, services, customers, and money truly work, both partners have to win. Many partnerships are formed between two organizations of vastly different sizes, so there is often a temptation to cut win–lose deals.

In 1990 United Parcel Service (UPS) and Mail Boxes Etc. cut a win–win deal.* Mail Boxes Etc. provides packing, shipping, receiving, secretarial, faxing, and photocopying services via retail storefronts. UPS invested about $11 million in the company; here's how both sides won:

- UPS got an instant nationwide network of convenient sites for customers to drop off and pick up packages. It didn't have to invest the time and money to build its own offices.
- Mail Boxes Etc. locked in UPS's business and averted the competition that would have occurred with UPS if it had decided to build its own offices.

The lopsidedness of many partnerships is not born of necessity. It usually occurs "just because" the larger entity can muscle the smaller one into a poor deal. This is a bad idea for both partners:

- Win–lose deals won't last. Oppression has seldom proven to be a sustainable system.
- If you want the middles and bottoms to support the partnership, both sides have to see the union as a win.
- It's bad karma, and karma counts for everything in a partnership.

If you're in a startup, be wary of entering into a win–lose partnership no matter how attractive the terms. They seldom work out. If you're in a big company, rein in your hormones and cut win–win partnerships. They are the only sustainable kind.

FOLLOW WITH THE FILE

Here's a nontheoretical question. Which comes first: a Kumbaya meeting of the minds or a draft of a legal document detailing the partnership? You can guess my bias.

---

*George Gendron, "A Sweet Deal," *Inc.*, March 1991.

Many entrepreneurs send a draft of the document as a straw man to get the discussion rolling. The thinking is that your organization is more nimble than the behemoth you're trying to partner with. You can move faster, so you'll do the drafting. Also, if you draft the document, then the other party has to start negotiating from your starting point, not theirs.

In fact, this is a high-risk approach because a document takes on a life of its own. It may, for example, be forwarded straight to an executive—or worse, a lawyer (see next section)—who wasn't informed that it was "just a starting point for our thinking." A document that's floating around can raise premature red flags that can derail the process.

Here's a better approach:

1. Get together face to face. Discuss the deal points.
2. When you start agreeing, go to a whiteboard and write them down.
3. Follow up with a one- to two-page e-mail outlining the "framework" for a partnership.
4. Reach closure on all details via e-mails, phone calls, and follow-up meetings.
5. Draft a legal document.

Many people try to go from Step 1 directly to Step 5—not a good idea. A document should always follow a discussion, never lead it.

WAIT TO LEGISLATE

For certain people, after fifty, litigation takes the place of sex.
—Gore Vidal

If there's one way to ensure that a partnership won't go through, it's asking for legal advice too early. If you do this, you'll learn that the number of reasons not to do a deal always exceeds the number of reasons to do it. The point is to agree on business terms *before* you bring in the lawyers. Then find a lawyer who genuinely wants to do deals, not prevent them, and set the right legal framework.

Many lawyers view their role as the "adult supervision" that will prevent stupid deals from taking place. However, their bias is often that a deal is bad until proven good. Avoid this kind of lawyer. Instead, find one who views his role as a problem solver and service function for you, the customer.

Having found the right lawyer, you need to establish this perspective: "Here is what I want to do. Now keep me out of jail." This is different from asking, "Can I do this?"

PUT AN "OUT" CLAUSE IN THE DEAL

As the Japanese (*sic*) say, "Mazel tov"—you've got the deal nearly done. Because everybody should win, the last thing in the world you want is for your partner to be able to end the arrangement, right?

Counterintuitive as this may seem, you should always be sure to include an out clause in the deal, something along the lines of "Either party can end this agreement upon thirty days' notice." The reason is that an easy "out" promotes the longevity of a deal because it assures both parties that they won't be trapped in an untenable predicament.

A safety like this enables everyone to chill out and work harder to make the partnership function—knowing that in the worst case, it's easy to end the deal. Also, people are more likely to take chances and be innovative when the partnership isn't set in stone.

Don't misunderstand me: I am not advocating partnerships that are easy to get out of. On the contrary, a good partnership involves the commitment of serious resources by both sides. However, it should be hard to get out of because of the importance of the partnership to both parties, not merely because of a contract.

GET OUT OF THE BELLY

In the words of Heidi Mason, coauthor of *The Venture Imperative*, trying to form a partnership with a larger, established organization is like being "stuck in the belly of a snake." You may get it done, but all you'll have left is a pile of bones. Thus, it's very important to recognize and interpret the top ten lies of partnering.

BIG ORGANIZATION SAYS . . .	YOU HEAR . . .
1. "We want to do this for strategic reasons."	They can't figure out how why this partnership is important.
2. "Our management really wants to do this."	A vice president heard about the proposal for thirty seconds and didn't have time to say no yet.
3. "We can move fast."	No one has talked to the legal department yet.
4. "Our legal department won't be a problem."	The legal department will be a huge problem.
5. "We want to time the announcement of our partnership with the release of a new version of our product."	The release will be late, and there's not a thing we can do about its delaying our partnership.
6. "The engineering team really likes it."	The marketing team is going to kill it.
7. "The marketing team really likes it."	The engineering team is going to kill it.
8. "The engineering and marketing teams really like it."	The lawyers are going to kill it.
9. "The engineering, marketing, and legal teams really like it."	Pinch yourself—you're asleep and dreaming.
10. "We're forming a cross-functional team to ensure the success of this project."	No one is accountable for the success of this project.

MINICHAPTER: THE ART OF SCHMOOZING

It's not what you know or who you know, but who knows you.

—Susan RoAne

It's much easier to build partnerships with people you already know—or, more accurately, with people who already know you. The process of building these social connections is called schmoozing.

If you're reticent about schmoozing—because you are shy or you consider it offensive or manipulative—you shouldn't be. In his book *The Frog and the Prince,* Darcy Rezac defines *networking* (which is "schmoozing" for goyim) as "discovering what you can do for someone else."*

World-class schmoozers adopt Rezac's outward, what-can-I-do-for-you attitude. It is the key to building extensive, long-lasting connections. Upon this foundation, here's how to get more people to know you:

- **GET OUT.** Schmoozing is a contact sport. You can't do it at home or in the office alone, so force yourself to attend trade shows, conventions, seminars, conferences, and cocktail receptions.

- **ASK GOOD QUESTIONS, THEN SHUT UP.** Good schmoozers don't dominate conversations. They start them off with interesting questions and then listen. Good schmoozers aren't good talkers; they are good listeners. No one is more fascinating than a good listener. The best opening question is "What do you do?"

- **FOLLOW UP.** Follow up within twenty-four hours of meeting someone. Send an e-mail. Give him a call. Send him a copy of your new book. Some people are afraid to give out their phone number or e-mail address because they fear they'll be inundated. That's never been my experience. So few people ever follow up that the ones who do are clearly special and worth knowing.

---

*Darcy Rezac, *The Frog and the Prince: Secrets of Positive Networking* (Vancouver: Frog and Prince Networking Corporation, 2003), 14.

- **MAKE IT EASY TO GET IN TOUCH.** This is ironic, but many people who want to be great schmoozers make it hard to contact them. For example, they don't carry business cards or don't print their e-mail address and phone number on them. If they do provide contact information, they don't respond to e-mail or voicemail.

- **UNVEIL YOUR PASSIONS.** If you can talk only about your business, you're a boring person. Good schmoozers are passionate about multiple and diverse interests. A benefit of these passions is that they provide additional ways to connect to people.

  I'm not saying you should take up a hobby because it will be good for business. For example, I'd rather be poor than play golf. However, I've made many business connections through hockey— and I've made many hockey connections through business.

  Just in case you don't like hockey, here are other points of passion through which we can connect: Audi cars, Breitling watches, tinnitus/Ménière's disease, boxers (the dog breed), adopting children, London, digital photography, and Macintosh. With these eight passions, I can connect to anyone in the world.

- **READ VORACIOUSLY.** If you're a pathetic person with no passions, then at least read voraciously so that you can talk a little about a lot of things. Set your home page to Google News (http://news.google. com/) to make this easier.

- **GIVE FAVORS.** There's a karmic scoreboard in the sky (more about this in Chapter 11, "The Art of Being a Mensch"). This scoreboard tracks what you do for people. If you want to be a world-class schmoozer, ensure that you're hugely positive on the scoreboard.

  You accomplish this by helping people—especially folks who seemingly can't do anything for you. And do this without expectation of return. Eventually, the scoreboard will take care of you.

- **RETURN FAVORS.** Since I believe in doing favors, I surely advocate returning favors. When something is done for you, you have accepted a moral obligation to pay it back. Great schmoozers return favors and do so with joy. This not only moves the scoreboard a little in the positive direction but enables you to ask for more favors.

- **ASK FOR THE RETURN OF FAVORS.*** Counterintuitive as this seems, you should ask for the return of favors. Doing so reduces or removes the pressure from a person who feels he owes you something. Thus, it provides an opportunity to clear the deck. Then the other party can ask for new favors.

MINICHAPTER: THE ART OF USING E-MAIL

I have made this [letter] longer, because I have not had the time to make it shorter.

—Blaise Pascal

E-mail is a key tool of a good schmoozer. It is fast, almost free, and ubiquitous. It's also poorly used by most people. Here's how to improve your e-mail effectiveness to make it a powerful schmoozing weapon:

- **FIX YOUR SUBJECT LINES AND NAME.** If people think your messages are spam, they won't read them. You may not be able to prevent spam filters from sorting out your messages, so be sure to use good subject lines to make it easy to see that they aren't spam.

  For example, "Follow-up to our meeting," "Enjoyed your speech," and "Nice to meet you in Kona" sure beat "Save on Viagra now!" "Increase your sales," or "Funds in Nigeria." Also, send yourself a message to see how the "from" line appears to a recipient. If your e-mail client software isn't sending out your properly capitalized first name and last name, fix this, too.

- **ANSWER WITHIN TWENTY-FOUR HOURS.** As I said before, responsiveness is a big factor in cementing a contact. You need to answer while the topic of the e-mail is fresh. Messages that are below the first screen of a person's inbox are often forgotten.

- **DON'T USE ALL CAPS.** All-caps text is more difficult to read, and it is considered "SHOUTING" at the reader. If nothing else, it's a sure sign that you're clueless about e-mail, and cluelessness is not conducive to successful schmoozing.

*Susan RoAne, *The Secrets of Savvy Networking* (New York: Warner Books, 1993), 56.

- **QUOTE BACK.** Select the question or section of the e-mail that you're responding to and quote it back so the sender knows what you're referring to. People get dozens of messages per day, so a simple "Yes, I agree," is not useful.

- **KEEP IT SHORT AND SIMPLE.** Cut the crap and get to it. The ideal length for an e-mail is fewer than five sentences. If you can't say what you have to say in five sentences, you don't have much to say.

  Use plain text, not HTML. I assume that all HTML e-mail is spam and have my e-mail client delete them automatically. If you have something significant to say, you don't need bold, outline, shadow, red text, and graphics to say it.

  Don't attach files unless you have permission. Imagine that your recipient is sitting in a hotel room making a slow phone connection, and you've sent a two-megabyte PowerPoint file. Do you think you'll get a positive reaction? Also, many people think attachments from strangers are viruses.

- **BLIND CARBON COPY (BCC) E-MAILS TO LARGE GROUPS.** As a rule of thumb, the more people you send an e-mail to, the fewer will respond. Thus, you should either reconsider whether everyone should get the e-mail or if you should conceal the list of recipients. When you send an e-mail to several people, it should always be a BCC to prevent inadvertent responses to everyone and to prevent revealing e-mail addresses to the other recipients.

- **REDUCE CARBON COPIES (CCs).** Either a person needs to get the e-mail or not. A CC is in the meaningless middle ground—it might be nice if the person were informed. The other heinous (and ineffective) uses of a CC are to cover one's butt ("But you were CCed!") or to threaten ("Look here! I CCed your boss."). When I get a CC, I assume that other people are taking care of the issue, and I ignore the e-mail.

- **INCLUDE A GOOD SIGNATURE.** A "signature" is several lines of text that your e-mail software automatically includes at the end of every outgoing message. A good signature provides your name, organization, postal address, phone and fax numbers, e-mail address, and Web site information. This is useful for copying and pasting into a calendar or database. God forbid someone should actually want to make more contact with you, and they have to hunt down the information. Here's what mine looks like:

Garage Technology Ventures
3300 Hillview, Suite 150
Palo Alto, CA 94304
650-354-1854
650-354-1801 (fax)
kawasaki@garage.com
www.garage.com

- **DON'T FORWARD SOMETHING YOU THINK IS FUNNY.** The odds are that your recipients have already gotten it ten times. If you generate something funny, more power to you. But if you're just forwarding a forward, spare your recipients.

- **WAIT WHEN YOU HATE.** Although you should generally answer e-mail in under twenty-four hours, there is one case where you should wait at least twenty-four hours before responding: when you're angry, offended, or argumentative. E-mail written when you're in these moods tends to exacerbate problems, so delay your response. It's even better to call when an issue is touchy because e-mail is a poor communicator of emotion and tone.

FAQ

Q. Since partnerships are supposed to be fifty–fifty, win–win situations, shouldn't the other party meet halfway in setting up meetings, moving the process along, getting its employees to cooperate, and so on?

A. "Should" and "will" are two different things. You're right that the other party should meet you halfway, but it probably won't. If you want a partnership, sale, or almost any transaction to happen, you've got to push for it. The other party may owe you a phone call or response, but don't just wait for it. Call again. You'll probably have to make 80 percent of the effort to bring something about, so swallow your pride.

Q. I've noticed that executives who are well established in their fields tend to resent a newcomer. There's a sense that I "haven't earned" the idea and that they should rightly have it because they were there first. How do I work with this attitude in potential partners?

A. Find others to partner with.

Q. How do I avoid being bullied by my contractual partners if they are larger, more established, and better funded than I am?

A. Never believe, or at least never act like you believe, that might makes right. For all you know, the elephant needs your product or service as much as you do. Go in there with a win–win attitude. If you encounter a win–lose attitude, and you can't change it, then don't do the deal.

Q. We're in some partnerships that aren't going anywhere. Should we invest the time and money to make them work or simply abandon them?

A. There's an old medical proverb that goes like this: "Nothing requires more heroic efforts than to keep a corpse from stinking, and yet nothing is quite so futile."* Focus your energies on partnerships that are working and new ones that have greater promise. But before you commit to new partnerships, figure out why the previous partnerships didn't pan out.

RECOMMENDED READING

Rezac, Darcy. *The Frog and the Prince: Secrets of Positive Networking.* Vancouver: Frog and Prince Networking Corporation, 2003.

RoAne, Susan. *The Secrets of Savvy Networking.* New York: Warner Books, 1993.

*Peter F. Drucker, *Innovation and Entrepreneurship: Practice and Principles* (New York: Harper & Row, 1985), 152.

CHAPTER 9

The Art of Branding

The best brands never start out with the intent of building a great brand.
They focus on building a great—and profitable—product or service and an
organization that can sustain it.
—Scott Bedbury

GIST

There are two major schools of thought regarding branding: The first holds that it's incomprehensible voodoo that marketers practice. I belong to the second, which contends that it's a simple matter of applying the classic Ps of marketing: product, place, price, and promotion.

To this list, some people have added another P: prayer. They are not far off—but instead of prayer, I prefer proselytization, which is the process of converting others to your belief, doctrine, or cause.

Proselytization, or evangelism, represents the core of branding for startups in today's highly competitive world, in which information is free, ubiquitous, and instantaneous. The art of branding requires creating something contagious that infects people with enthusiasm, making it easy for them to try it, asking them for help in spreading the word, and building a community around it.

Though I love marketing, great brands start with a great product or service, so that's where we'll start, too.

CREATE A CONTAGION

I call it "Guy's Golden Touch." It's not the vainglorious concept that whatever I touch turns to gold, but rather, simply and more humbly, "Whatever is gold, Guy touches."

Herein lies the secret to branding: Align with a product or service that's gold—or enhance it until it *is* gold. Then successful branding is easy if not unavoidable. How hard do you think it was to brand Macintosh in 1984 when the competition was butt-ugly and boring?

If you have something that's gold, you can make a lot of mistakes with it and still succeed. If you don't, you have to do almost everything right. So make it easy on yourself and create or find products and services that are inherently contagious. These are the key elements of contagiousness:

- **COOL.** Cool is beautiful. Cool is hip. Cool is idiosyncratic. And cool is contagious. Few companies purposely design products and services that aren't cool, but we continue to see hundreds of eye-numbing efforts. Why did it take Apple to ship an MP3 player as cool as the iPod?

- **EFFECTIVE.** You can't brand crap. You can't brand something that doesn't work. No one would have heard of TiVo if it didn't almost effortlessly record the television shows you wanted.

- **DISTINCTIVE.** A contagious product is easy to notice and advertises itself. It leaves no doubt that it is different from the competition. Does anyone confuse a Hummer with other vehicles?

- **DISRUPTIVE.** Contagious products are disruptive. They either upset the status quo ("Oh, hell, this is better. We're in trouble.") or make them go into denial ("Why would anyone want a graphical user interface?"). But they do not leave people unaffected.

- **EMOTIVE.** A contagious product or service exceeds expectations, and by exceeding expectations, it makes you joyful. This is how I feel about our Miele vacuum cleaner—I'm amazed that it can suck so hard yet make so little noise.*

- **DEEP.** A contagious product or service "has legs." The more you use it, the more you discover it is capable of. Going back to TiVo, if you want to skip through advertising, enter this keystroke sequence: Select, Play, Select, 30, Select. Then, pressing the key that takes you to the end of a recorded program (−−>|) will now make you jump ahead in thirty-second intervals.

- **INDULGENT.** Purchasing a contagious product or service makes you feel as if you've indulged yourself. This may be because it costs more than the alternatives, it's cooler, or it's more than you really need. Thus, it enables you to escape the mundane. The tag line for Miele, for example, is "Anything else is a compromise."

- **SUPPORTED.** Providing exemplary service makes a product or service contagious. I once broke a medical device that treats my ear problems. The manufacturer, Medtronic Xomed, sent me a loaner via overnight delivery at no charge. It also repaired and shipped out my unit on the same day that the unit was received—also at no charge. And that day was a national holiday. Finally, in a bold stroke of accountability and personal touches, Medtronic provided the name, e-mail address, and digital photo of the technician who fixed it on the packing slip. Do you think I recommend this product to others with similar ear problems?

EXERCISE

The next time you get technical support from a company, ask the person for his name, e-mail address, and photo.

---

*As opposed to people—the ones who suck the most are the noisiest.

LOWER THE BARRIERS TO ADOPTION

An innovation, to be effective, has to be simple and it has to be focused. It should do only one thing, otherwise, it confuses. If it is not simple, it won't work.

—Peter Drucker

Lowering the barriers to adoption is a theme that has been repeated often in this book. It applies to making it rain as well as to branding. The more prevalent your product or service, the more likely you'll build a big brand.

A Chinese pharmaceutical company named Kunming illustrates what not to do. This company was determined to make a childproof aspirin bottle, so it created one that had thirteen moving parts and took thirty-nine steps to open. For added safety, the company changed the design every six months. The problem was that its intended customers couldn't open the bottle. Ironically, the company discovered that adults were buying the pills and giving the bottles to kids as puzzles.*

The most common barrier that startups erect, however unintentionally, is complexity. Sure, if 1 percent of the people in China bought your aspirin because of the safety feature in the bottle, you'd achieve a lot of sales. But if it takes too long to learn how to use your product (or to open its bottle) or service, you're making it harder to build a brand.

Few companies set out to create a complex and difficult-to-use product or service, but you have to wonder why so many products have such an incomprehensible interface. Almost anything from Japanese consumer electronics manufacturers, for example, illustrates this point. (They then compound the problem with an unreadable, broken-English manual printed in four-point gray type.) Here are ways to reduce complexity:

---

*Brad Schreiber, *Weird Wonders and Bizarre Blunders: The Official Book of Ridiculous Records* (Deephaven, MN: Meadowbrook Press, 1989), 17.

- **FLATTEN THE LEARNING CURVE.** A customer should be able to get basic functionality right "out of the box" without having to turn to a manual. Imagine if you bought a car and had to read the manual to turn on its radio, change the station, and increase the volume. Mandate this to your designers: Customers must get immediate gratification without opening a manual.

- **WRITE A GOOD MANUAL AND INDEX IT THOROUGHLY.** Typically, an underpaid person down in the bowels of an organization writes a product's or service's manual at the last possible moment. The manual isn't tested, and it's laid out in a tiny font with out-of-date illustrations.

  Your manual is a marketing opportunity. It is a window onto the soul of your product or service! The better the manual, the more people will enjoy using your product or service. This in turn fosters more good word-of-mouth branding.

  If manual writing is at the bottom of the totem pole, manual indexing is under the ground. Have you ever tried to determine the correct tire pressure for your car, and been unable to find "tire pressure" listed in the manual's index?

  Think of every possible thing a customer will want to do with your product and make sure there's an entry for it in the index. If you want to see an example of a great index, look at the index in *The Chicago Manual of Style*. It contains approximately forty page references to the topic of dashes! Hold your organization to this standard. (FYI: I indexed *The Art of the Start*.)

- **INCLUDE PICTURES.** One more thing about manuals: Add pictures and diagrams. This might increase the cost of your manuals, but it's well worth it. Not every user is text-centric. Pictures do count for a thousand words.

EXERCISE

Run a contest asking your customers to write the best manual for your product or service. You'll have a handful of good manuals, and you'll uncover some evangelists.

- **TEST IT ON YOUR MOTHER OR FATHER.** Ageist as this may seem, the ultimate test of a new product or service is seeing if your parents can use it. If your mother and father are no longer alive, try it on anyone over forty-five years old.

  Do not, however, attempt this with teenagers—they can figure out anything, so their feedback is irrelevant. If you want free, word-of-mouth brand building, spend the time and energy to create a user interface that a mere mortal can comprehend.

In addition to complexity, a high price is also a barrier to building a brand. To avoid this, when Toyota introduced its Lexus line of luxury cars, it priced them far lower than the German competition. Because the cars were less expensive, there were more owners out there. Since there were more owners, it was easy to find someone to talk to about them and learn how great they were.

I hate competing on price and leaving money on the table. However, squeezing every penny out of your customer is usually not the right philosophy, either. A reasonable price that fosters the creation of a brand can produce larger returns later.

EXERCISE

Which company would you rather own: Toyota or Rolls-Royce?

The final common barrier to adoption is the cost of converting (measured in money, time, or effort) from an existing product or service to your new one. Your product or service can be cheap, and it can be easy to use, but if it's painful to switch to, you're making branding more difficult.

Branding aside, it makes good sense to make converting as easy as possible. Few companies would make it difficult to convert from an existing product to their product on purpose, but few companies seem to realize that a lower conversion cost is good marketing.

Finally, you might think that making it hard to switch *from* your product is a good idea. This is a way to lock in your customer, but exit barriers are also entry barriers. If you make it hard to switch from your product, you'll also scare people from trying your product in the first place.

RECRUIT EVANGELISTS

Evangelists believe in your product or service as much as you do, and they want to carry the battle forward for you and with you. Recruiting evangelists can help you achieve critical mass through sustained, continuous, and low-cost proselytization and branding. If you are involved in politics, not-for-profits, schools, and churches, evangelism is an especially powerful tool to achieve success.

When it comes to evangelism, it's not true that "if you don't ask, you don't get." When your product, service, or idea is contagious and there are low barriers around it, you often "get" without asking. But if you do ask, you can get much more, much faster. However, many companies hesitate to ask because of thinking like this:

- "If we ask for help, people will think we're weak. A strong company like Microsoft never asks its customers for help."
- "The people we ask will expect something in return: discounts, special treatment, etc. Then what will we do?"
- "Our customers, much as we love them, can't help us. We know what to do, and we can do it ourselves."
- "It will cost too much to maintain special support programs. They'll defocus our efforts."

These reasons are bogus. When customers want to help you, you should rejoice, not restrain them, so stifle your paranoia and accept the help. The customers will turn into evangelists who spread your good news.

Following are the keys principles of recruiting evangelists. You'll notice several similarities to concepts in Chapter 6 ("The Art of Recruiting"), which is no accident. In a sense, you are recruiting "employees"—you just don't need to pay these folks.

- **ASK!** Go to your early and best customers and ask for help. Tell them you want to achieve critical mass, and that you need to spread the word. This isn't a sign of weakness—it is a sign of openness and aggressiveness. You'll be amazed at the number of people who are willing to help, and who have been waiting to be asked.

- **IGNORE ACADEMIC BACKGROUND AND WORK EXPERIENCE.** (Very) theoretically, the best evangelist for a software product might be someone with a Ph.D. in computer science from MIT. Avoid this type of thinking. Track records mean little when it comes to evangelism. The greatest Macintosh evangelists never used a computer before they bought one.

- **FOCUS ON WHAT'S IMPORTANT: DO THEY BELIEVE, AND DO THEY WANT TO HELP?** Take someone (me, for example) who twenty years ago had never had a computer class in his life and whose then-current job was schlepping diamonds. Would he be the ideal candidate to evangelize a new operating system? Looking back, what mattered most was that I loved Macintosh and wanted to change the world with it.

- **LET A HUNDRED EVANGELISTS BLOSSOM.** This is another recurring theme of this book: Don't be picky about how evangelists help you. Show them your product or service and let them work for you in any way they can. They will show you ways to market your product and services that you never would have developed yourself.

- **ASSIGN TASKS AND EXPECT THEM TO GET DONE.*** Have you ever volunteered to help an organization and then never been called to action? If there's anything worse than being asked to do something you don't want to, it's not being asked to do something you do. If you've gotten this far with evangelists, they've signed up for the cause. Now it's your obligation to make good use of them.

- **CONTINUE "FELLOWSHIP."†** The model for effective evangelism is the relationship between a good parent and child. As any parent

---

*Brad Schreiber, *Weird Wonders and Bizarre Blunders: The Official Book of Ridiculous Records* (Deephaven, MN: Meadowbrook Press, 1989,) 92–93.
†Ibid., 47.

will tell you, your kids will always be your kids. They never truly leave the nest, and you certainly don't push them out of it. Evangelists are the same—they need frequent and perpetual lovin'.

- **GIVE THEM THE TOOLS TO EVANGELIZE.** Make it easy for believers to help you by providing stacks of information and promotional material. For example, Bose includes ten "courtesy cards" in the Bose QuietComfort 2 Acoustic Noise Cancelling Headphones case for owners to pass out to people who ask them about the product. The card explains how to find out more about the product, purchase it, and get more cards by calling a toll-free number!

**QuietComfort® 2
Acoustic Noise Cancelling®
Headphones**

Courtesy Card

Our customers tell us they are often asked about their Bose®QuietComfort®2 Acoustic Noise Cancelling® headphones. For your convenience, we are providing this handy courtesy card for you to pass along.

For more information or to purchase a headphone, please call:

United States: 1-800-372-2673 ext. Q1896
Outside the US: 508-766-1942

United Kingdom: 08000 85 85 72, ref. 7212
Outside the UK: +44 1392 428 361

BOSE www.bose.com/q1904

For additional courtesy cards, please call: 1-888-865-2700

257641 AM Rev.00

- **RESPOND TO THEIR DESIRES.** You should revise your product or service to reflect the wishes of your evangelists for two reasons. First, they will be among the most knowledgeable about what it takes to make it better. Second, and as important, demonstrating that you do listen to them will foster even greater loyalty and enthusiasm for helping you.

- **GIVE THEM STUFF.** You would be amazed at the power of a free T-shirt, coffee mug, pen, or notepad. (At one point, Apple had a $2 million per year T-shirt expense.) Evangelists love these goodies. It makes them feel like they're part of the team and special. This is money well spent, but never give away anything that costs more than $25. A Montblanc pen, for example, is over the line and will make you look like you're wasting money.

Let's assume that you are successful in recruiting customers to be evangelists. What should you ask them to do? That is the topic of the next section.

FOSTER A COMMUNITY

In the late 1990s, a group of business people and community leaders started an organization called the Calgary Flames Ambassadors. They were Flames fans who were alarmed by the prospect that their National Hockey League team might move to another city. According to the chairman of the group, Lyle Edwards, "The Ambassadors ran around Calgary and twisted arms so that people bought more tickets."

Circa 2004, the group had fifty members, and they don't have to help sell tickets anymore. To join the Ambassadors, you have to buy a season ticket and pay $100 Canadian to the Ambassadors organization. That's right: these evangelists pay for the privilege of proselytizing the Flames. They greet fans at games, promote community outreach, and conduct social events.

The goal of recruiting evangelists is to build a community around your product or service. Examples of companies that enjoy well-publicized communities include Apple, Harley-Davidson, Motley Fool, and Saturn. These communities provide customer service, technical support, and social relationships that make owning a product or utilizing a service a better experience—they also twist arms so that people buy more products, services, or tickets.

Surprisingly, most companies *react* to the formation of communities *after* they appear, and their reaction is: "Never heard of them . . . You mean to say that there are groups of customers who get together because of our product?"

This is suboptimal, if not downright stupid. Having seen how some companies have benefited from the spontaneous generation of communities, you should proactively bring one into existence:

- **IDENTIFY AND RECRUIT THE "THUNDER LIZARDS" OF YOUR PRODUCT OR SERVICE.** These are the customers who are the most enthusiastic about what you do and who are willing to serve in leadership positions.

- **HIRE SOMEONE WHOSE SOLE PURPOSE IS TO FOSTER A COMMUNITY.** This is your internal champion for the needs of the community; he evangelizes evangelists and fights for internal resources. As you achieve success, build a department around this person to institutionalize community support.

- **CREATE A BUDGET FOR COMMUNITY SUPPORT.** You won't need much, and the intent is not for you to "buy" a community. But you'll still need a budget for the community to hold meetings, print and circulate newsletters, and maintain an online presence.

- **INTEGRATE THE PRESENCE OF THE COMMUNITY INTO YOUR SALES AND MARKETING EFFORTS AND YOUR ONLINE PRESENCE.** For example, your Web site should provide information about the community, including instructions for joining it.

- **HOST THE COMMUNITY'S EFFORTS.** This means letting members use your building to hold meetings as well as providing digital assistance, such as operating an e-mail listserver, online chat, and bulletin board on your Web site.

- **HOLD A CONFERENCE.** No one loves electronic communication more than I do, but face-to-face meetings are important for communities. At these conferences, community members can meet one another as well as interact with your own employees.

Per dollar, building a community of customers and evangelists is the cheapest method for creating and maintaining a brand, so don't screw up by waiting for a community to form on its own.

EXERCISE

Look at the back of this book's dust jacket. Can you figure out why we printed so many cover design entries?

ACHIEVE HUMANNESS

Consider several great brands: Apple, Coca-Cola, Levi Strauss, Nike, and Saturn. They've all achieved humanness: the funkiness of Apple, the joy of Coca-Cola, the youthfulness of Levi Strauss, the gutsy determination of Nike, and the buddy-buddy feeling of Saturn.

To be sure, there are great brands that don't exhibit these qualities—Microsoft, Oracle, and IBM, to name a few. Call me a romantic, but wouldn't it be better and more fun to have a warm brand? If you agree, here's how to achieve this:

- **TARGET THE YOUNG.** No matter who actually buys your product or service, targeting young people forces you to build a warm brand. I have no data to back this up, but it seems that lots of old people are buying products that were initially targeted to young people. For example, check out how many bald heads are driving Toyota Scions, PT Cruisers, and Mini Coopers.

- **MAKE FUN OF YOURSELF.** Most companies are incapable of having a sense of humor about themselves, an attitude they view as suicidal: "People won't take us seriously if we don't take ourselves seriously." Or, they are so caught up in their self-image that appearing to lack total control scares them. As the saying goes, "To err is human," so don't be afraid to err and to make fun of that error.

- **FEATURE YOUR CUSTOMERS.** Organizations that feature their customers in marketing materials exude humanness. For example, Saturn features the owners of its cars in its marketing materials. Saturn's Web site even features an area called "My Story," in which customers discuss their Saturn experiences.

- **HELP THE UNDERSERVED AND UNDERPRIVILEGED.** An organization that supports the underserved and underprivileged communicates humanness. Hallmark Cards, for example, provides money and volunteers to many community programs. There's an easy-to-find section of their Web site about how to apply for such resources. This is a double win: Not only are you fulfilling a moral obligation to the community, you are also furthering the effectiveness of your brand.

EXERCISE

Go to the Web sites of your favorite companies and try to find information about how to apply for grants and volunteer for the company.

FOCUS ON PUBLICITY

For weeks before the debut of the Ikea store in East Palo Alto, California, residents of the area read story after story about its grand opening. For example, a story by Thaai Walker in the August 14, 2003, edition of the *San Jose Mercury News* started this way:

> CAR-GO HELP FOR IKEA SHOPPERS
> CITY BRACES FOR OPENING DAY TRAFFIC

> How do you move 16,000 shoppers packed into 8,000 cars through a 2.5-square-mile city on a day when the biggest, bluest store to grace East Palo Alto's horizon opens to the public?

If you read any local newspaper, listened to the radio, or watched television, it was impossible not to learn that Ikea was opening a new branch in East Palo Alto, and it was going to be a huge event.

Brands such as Ikea are not built on advertising. Advertising may maintain and expand brands, but it's publicity that establishes them. Here are the key concepts of attracting publicity and press coverage:

- **CREATE BUZZ, GET INK.** Most organizations think that press coverage generates buzz as readers clamor to become customers. This is backward thinking. Here's how it works: First, you create something grand. Then you lower the barriers to adoption and get it into the hands of people. They, in turn, generate buzz. Then the press will write about it.

- **MAKE FRIENDS BEFORE YOU NEED THEM.** When I worked for Apple, the press always wanted to interview "Apple execs" because it was a hot company. During such heady and flattering times, the temptation is always to focus on the important publications: *The New York Times, The Wall Street Journal, Forbes,* etc.

  I gravitated instead toward helping reporters from publications that you would never have heard of. Years later, these reporters are now at the important publications, and they remember how I helped them. The lesson is "Make friends before you need them—and even before they can help you."

- **USE A RIFLE, NOT A SHOTGUN.** My reporter friends tell me that organizations often "shotgun" their newsrooms—meaning that every reporter in the news department gets a press kit or e-mail about some miraculous new product or service. This approach rarely works because your material will be irrelevant to almost all the recipients.

  Instead, first determine if your story is appropriate for the publication. Fascinating as you might find it, it might not be. Mitch Betts, features editor of *ComputerWorld,* described whom he would recommend contact his publication: "If CIOs of General Motors, Wal-Mart, Amazon would be interested, we'd be interested."* That's how relevant you need to be.

  Second, determine which reporter covers your specific area—for example, pitching the arts reporter about a new enterprise's software package isn't going to bear any fruit.

---

*Found at http://www.marketingsherpa.com/sample.cfm?contentID=2420.

Third, pitch that particular reporter only if your story can pass an important test: "Is it good and useful for the readers?" The test is not "Is it good for our organization?" Believe it or not, publications exist for their readers, not as vehicles for your marketing.

- **BE A FOUL-WEATHER FRIEND.** Many organizations kiss up to journalists when things are going great and they want coverage. But when things turn bad or busy, they disappear on them by not returning phone calls and e-mails. No matter what the weather, you must maintain good relations with the press.

- **TELL THE TRUTH.** When things go bad, there's a temptation to lie to the press to get out of a jam. Don't do it. You establish your credibility during bad times, not good. Anyone can tell the truth when things are going well. If you've established a record for being honest when times are bad, the press will believe you when times are good.

- **BE A SOURCE.** Sometimes your story isn't worth covering, or there is no place to mention your organization in the reporter's story. That's OK. At these times, simply be a source and help the journalist write a good story. Your turn will come.

TALK THE WALK

Hidden Villa is a 1,600-acre farm and wilderness preserve in Los Altos, California. The Josephine and Frank Duveneck family gave it to the people of Northern California to foster environmental and multicultural awareness. Its programs include summer camps, environmental education, community outreach, hostel accommodations, and organic farming.

In short, Hidden Villa "walks the talk"—that is, it makes enormous meaning for the community and delivers on its goals. (This contrasts sharply to the behavior of many organizations, which talk a good game but do not deliver results.) However, the organization noticed that its employees and directors didn't have the tools to promote it in a concise and compelling way.

To fix this problem, the organization created a program called "Talk the Walk," which involved developing one-liners that explain

Hidden Villa. Then, at an offsite, members of the Hidden Villa staff and directors role-played using these one-liners. Now they are all able to "talk the walk" whether they are at a Hidden Villa event or bumping into a friend in the supermarket.

The starting point for branding is inside your organization, so make sure that every employee can "talk the walk" and enthusiastically proselytize the organization.

MINICHAPTER: THE ART OF SPEAKING

Why is it that those who have something to say can't say it, while those who have nothing to say keep saying it?

—anonymous

"Pitching" typically refers to making a presentation to potential investors, customers, and partners in a small, informal meeting at the prospect's office. In addition to pitching, there will be opportunities to give speeches and to participate on panels at conferences, seminars, and industry events. These are useful vehicles to build awareness for your organization.

The purpose of these appearances is not to raise money (though a good speech can generate interest in investing) but to increase awareness of the organization and build a brand. I've seen dozens of executives give speeches and participate on panels, and, with rare exceptions, they suck. This happens for the following reasons:

- Executives are surrounded by minions who don't have the knowledge, courage, or competence to tell the emperor that he has no clothes.

- Executives are egomaniacs. They have lofty self-images, so they cannot believe that they are not dynamite speakers right out of the womb.

- Executives are busy people who have little time to practice—or, more accurately, who *allocate* little time to practice. The combination of denying the need to practice and not having the time to do it is the kiss of death.

First, let's cover the principles of giving an effective speech. This opportunity is a powerful weapon because you have the podium all to yourself. You can, for the most part, control the entire block of time.

- **SAY SOMETHING INTERESTING.** This is an obvious but widely ignored point. If you don't have something interesting to say, don't speak. If you don't speak, people won't know you're a loser. If you do speak, you'll leave no doubt. Better the former than the latter.

- **OVERDRESS.** In contrast to when making a pitch, it is better to be overdressed than underdressed. An audience interprets casual dress as your saying, "You're not important enough to make any effort." If you overdress, the worst-case scenario is that you'll look too professional.

- **CUT THE SALES PROPAGANDA.** People attend a speech because they want information, not to get a blatant sales pitch. Logical or not, an audience tends to think that good speakers have good products and services. If you inform them with a high-content and relevant speech, they might buy. If you sales-pitch them, they won't.

- **TELL STORIES.** For some people, making an interesting speech is harder than upgrading Microsoft Windows. Great speakers don't simply make assertions, they tell stories. Make a point, tell a story to illustrate it, make another point, and tell a story to illustrate it.

- **CIRCULATE WITH THE CROWD BEFORE YOU SPEAK.** I give fifty keynotes a year, and I find it tremendously encouraging to see people in the audience whom I've already met. A few friendly faces give me the confidence to make a bolder speech. The goal is to recruit some friends who will be the first to laugh at your jokes, nod in agreement with your insights, and applaud your performance.

- **TALK ABOUT KIDS.** If there's a surefire way to endear yourself to an audience, it's to talk about your kids. If you don't have kids, talk about your relative's kids, your friend's kids, or when you were a kid. I've never seen an audience that doesn't appreciate a good kid story.

- **SELF-DEPRECATE.** Another good way to win over an audience is to make fun of yourself. If you're nervous, mention that you're nervous. Most people in the crowd will empathize with you. If you can't find one thing to make fun of about yourself, you're either a total bore or a total orifice.

- **SPEAK AT THE START OF AN EVENT.** If you're given a choice, speak on the first day of the conference. That's when attendance and energy are at their highest, and therefore it's the easiest atmosphere in which to give a good speech. By the last day, many people will have departed, and those who remain are probably out of gas, which means you have to devote some of your time to lifting them out of their lethargy. Giving a good speech is hard enough without this added pressure.

- **ASK FOR A SMALL ROOM.** If you can, speak in a small, crowded room. Audience energy is a function of how full the room is, not the absolute number of people in the audience. For example, 250 people in a 250-capacity room is much better than 500 people in a 1,000-capacity room. If you can't get a small room, try asking for a classroom-style layout (tables and chairs) rather than theater-style layout (chairs only).

- **FIND OUT WHAT HAPPENED EARLIER AT THE EVENT.** This is another reason why it's good to go on first: You don't have to learn what happened before you. In fact, you can be the "event" that other speakers have to cope with.

  However, if you're not the first speaker, try to attend the sessions that precede you, or at least ask your hosts if anything dramatically good, bad, or funny has already occurred. Then weave this incident into your speech. This accomplishes two things: First, it increases the perception that you customized your talk; second, it shows that you care enough about the event that you've been there for a while.

- **DON'T DENIGRATE THE COMPETITION.** It is a privilege and an honor to give a speech. Your duty is to inform and entertain the audience. This is not an opportunity to slash and burn your competition. Doing so will reflect poorly on you, not on your competition, and will create the opposite effect of what you intended.

- **PRACTICE.** As a rule of thumb, the twenty-fifth time you give a speech is when it gets good. Few people will practice or give the same speech twenty-five times. That's why there are so few good speakers. Ironically, the more you practice, the more you'll sound spontaneous.

- **USE A TOP-TEN LIST FORMAT.** I use a top-ten list format so that an audience can track progress through my speeches. Few experts agree with this, but I urge you to try it. If you can't come up with ten interesting things to say about a subject, then don't speak.

Next, let's discuss appearances on panels. Panels are excellent opportunities to build a brand because they allow you to position against others—frequently competitors—on the panel. Here's how to be a great panelist.

- **CONTROL YOUR INTRODUCTION.** Bring a copy of your bio and hand it to the moderator who will introduce you. Don't depend on what the moderator comes up with. And, as in speeches, cut the sales pitch about your organization. To make your organization look good, be an informative panelist, not a loudmouth braggart.

- **ENTERTAIN, DON'T JUST INFORM.** Answering the moderator's or audience's questions is only half the job of a panelist. The more important task is to entertain the audience. You can do this with penetrating new insight, humor, or controversy. Always ask yourself, *Am I being entertaining?*

- **TELL THE TRUTH—ESPECIALLY WHEN THE TRUTH IS OBVIOUS.** Most people expect panelists to lie when they encounter a tough question, so if you don't lie, you establish credibility for your other answers.

- **ERR ON THE SIDE OF BEING PLAIN AND SIMPLE.** Often a moderator will ask a technical question, so the temptation is to respond with a technical answer. This is usually a mistake. Keep it plain and simple: enough to show that you know what you're talking about but not so much that it makes you incomprehensible to 80 percent of the audience.

- **NEVER LOOK BORED.** You can look happy, sad, angry (at what's being said, not that you have to be on the panel), or incredulous, but never look bored. Someone in the audience will be looking at you, a photographer will snap a picture, or a videocameraman will focus on you. Unfortunately, you are most likely to be bored when other panelists are talking, so learn how to fake interest.

- **DON'T LOOK AT THE MODERATOR.** Play to the audience, not the moderator; the audience wants to see the front of your face, not its side. A good moderator will purposely not look at you or draw your eye contact.

- **MAKE CASUAL CONVERSATION.** You're onstage, but act as if you're not. Simply make conversation with the moderator and other panelists. Don't pontificate and don't "make a speech." Interact with everyone (even the audience) in a casual way.

- **ANSWER THE QUESTION POSED, BUT NEVER LIMIT YOURSELF TO THE QUESTION POSED.** For example, if you're asked, "Is file intrusion detection an important technology?," don't just say no. Say, "No, but let me tell you what is really hot." Most panelists go to one of two extremes: answering only the question or providing an answer that had nothing to do with the question.

- **NEVER SAY, "I AGREE WITH WHAT THE OTHER PANELISTS HAVE SAID."** Just say something different or new. If the other panelists have said everything you want to say (which is unlikely), be gracious: "Everything has been said. Let's move on out of respect for the audience." It's usually better to appear considerate rather than stupid.

MINI-MINICHAPTER: THE ART OF DESIGNING T-SHIRTS

The person who is waiting for something to turn up might start with their shirt sleeves.

—Garth Henrichs

Making T-shirts to announce a product or company is a fine Silicon Valley tradition, perfected by Apple back in the mid-eighties. We'd print and distribute the T-shirts, then announce the product, and then start development.

When we launched Garage in 1997, our first product was a T-shirt for kids that said, "I'm a little entrepreneur. My favorite letters are I, P, and O." We sold hundreds of them—being the e-commerce pioneers that we were.

In an attempt to build a brand and create a desirable tchotchke, many organizations print T-shirts. Unfortunately, many are downright ugly and scream, "We're dweebs with no sense of design!" Honestly, T-shirts aren't a big part of building a brand, but if you're going to do it, do it right.

- **DON'T USE WHITE SHIRTS.** White quickly turns to gray because people don't segregate their laundry like they should. If you use white, you'll significantly reduce the chest life of the T-shirt because few people like to wear dingy clothes.

- **MINIMIZE TEXT.** Think of a T-shirt as a moving billboard. People don't put paragraphs of text on a billboard. Follow the same rules for T-shirts. Use no more than six to ten words. At Garage, we printed a shirt that said, "Startup, kick butt, cash out."

- **USE A BIG (SIXTY-POINT) FONT.** The purpose of a company T-shirt is to publicize something. If you use a twelve-point font, no one will be able to read the text. If you can't read a T-shirt from twenty feet, the design is wrong.

- **SPEND A FEW BUCKS ON DESIGN.** T-shirts are an art form. If all you're going to do is slap on some text, don't even bother. This is especially true if you want women to wear them. Make your T-shirts bold and beautiful—go for it. It's only a shirt, after all.

- **MAKE THEM IN KID'S SIZES.** Some adults won't wear T-shirts— it's beneath their fashion standards (though you sure couldn't tell by looking at them). However, they don't care what their kids wear, and kids prefer them, anyway.

FAQ

Q. Should I advertise or depend exclusively on evangelism, buzz, and word-of-mouth?

A. In his book *The Anatomy of Buzz*, Emanuel Rosen provides a fine explanation of the relationship between advertising and guerilla marketing techniques. He unequivocally believes that advertising is an important part of branding. His reasons include jump-starting the process of buzz, reaching hubs of opinion leaders, reassuring customers, and providing the facts.* He goes on to discuss how advertising can both stimulate buzz and kill it. His book is well worth buying.

If you have to pick only one set of techniques, use the guerilla ones. But if you have the resources, do both.

Q. Do I need a PR firm? Or a PR department?

A. The answer is the same for a PR firm and an internal PR department. Here's what they can do: force you to create a solid branding message; open the door for you with members of the press via preexisting relationships; schedule meetings and interviews and make sure that you're presentable; provide postinterview feedback; and help you improve your meeting and presentation skills. Here's what they cannot do: take second-rate products and services and generate countless articles about them; make the company always look good; and prevent the company from ever looking bad.

Here's what they should never do: become the thought police through which external communications and branding must pass for "approval."

Q. Should I pay evangelists for their help?

A. No. They're not evangelizing your product or service for the money. They're doing it as a way to make the world a better place. You might, in fact, insult them by trying to pay them. The three best forms of compensation you can provide are to make your product or service better, to offer stacks of information and documentation, and to honor them publicly.

Q. Is it important to build a brand in our local area or start immediately with international exposure?

---

*Emanuel Rosen, *The Anatomy of Buzz: How to Create Word-of-Mouth Marketing* (New York: Doubleday/Currency, 2000), 206–9.

A. Generally, you should establish your product and service—and therefore your brand—locally before you venture forth. It's much better to establish your brand solidly in a small area than to have it almost established in many areas.

However, you may have the type of product or service where customers are spread out around the world, and their commonality isn't geographic but based on other parameters. This is OK, too. The point is to go deep before you go broad—along whatever parameter "deep" appears.

Q. What if we realize that we have a stinker of a branding concept, or we want to change our direction in the middle of a branding campaign?

A. Here are several thoughts, perhaps conflicting, for you. First, I don't believe in "branding campaigns," a term that implies that branding is a short-term project. It's not. Branding is continuous and perpetual.

Second, how did you decide it's a stinker? Do you want to change because you're tired of your logo, look and feel, tag line, mantra . . . whatever? Because typically it's about the time that you are getting tired of these things that the public is just getting them into their skulls.

Third, if you're not achieving revenues, the problem is probably something more fundamental, such as an inferior product or service.

Fourth, if your product or service is fundamentally good, and you truly have a mispositioned brand, do make a change. Ask the people who are buying your product or service what it stands for—this is usually a great start for effective branding.

RECOMMENDED READING

Aaker, David. *Managing Brand Equity: Capitalizing on the Value of a Brand Name.* New York: Free Press, 1991.

Bedbury, Scott. *A New Brand World: 8 Principles for Achieving Brand Leadership in the 21st Century.* New York: Viking, 2002.

Borden, Richard. *Public Speaking—as Listeners Like It!* New York: Harper & Brothers, 1935. (This book is seriously out of print, but I found a copy at Amazon.com.)

Gladwell, Malcolm. *The Tipping Point: How Little Things Can Make a Big Difference.* Boston: Little, Brown, 2000.

Nielsen, Jacob, et al. *E-Commerce User Experience*. Fremont, CA: Nielsen Norman Group, 2001.

Norman, Donald. *The Design of Everyday Things*. New York: Doubleday/Currency, 1988.

Ries, Al, and Laura Ries. *The 22 Immutable Laws of Branding: How to Build a Product or Service into a World-Class Brand*. New York: HarperBusiness, 2002.

Rosen, Emanuel. *The Anatomy of Buzz: How to Create Word-of-Mouth Marketing*. New York: Doubleday/Currency, 2000.

CHAPTER 10

The Art of Rainmaking

Stop going for the easy buck and start producing something with your life. Create, instead of living off the buying and selling of others.

—Carl Fox (in the movie *Wall Street*)

GIST

A Native American rainmaker is a medicine man who uses rituals and incantations to make it rain. For startups, a rainmaker is a person who generates large quantities of business. Like medicine men, entrepreneurs have created their own rituals and incantations to make it rain.

Two factors make rainmaking difficult for startups. First, although entrepreneurs design a product or service for a specific purpose, they have no way of knowing who will actually buy it and what it will be used for. Thus, the first step of rainmaking is to get version 1.0 of the product or service into the marketplace to find out where it blossoms. Keep your eyes open because you may find yourself in the midst of a gorilla market.

Second, the products and services of startups are rarely just bought. Instead, they must be sold because few customers want to take a chance on a new product or service from a small, undercapitalized organization. Thus, the second step of rainmaking is to overcome this resistance.

Before we begin, here's a story that illustrates how an entrepreneur both found out who would buy her product and overcame resistance to stocking it. A Parisian store once rejected the newest fragrance of Estée Lauder, the famed purveyor of perfume. In anger, Lauder poured the fragrance all over the floor, and so many customers asked about it that the store had to carry it. Sometimes when it pours, it rains.*

LET ONE HUNDRED FLOWERS BLOSSOM

I stole this concept from Mao Tse-tung, although he didn't exactly implement it during the Cultural Revolution. In the context of startups, the concept means

> Sow many seeds. See what takes root and then blossoms. Nurture those markets.

Many companies freak out when they notice that unintended flowers have started blossoming. They react by trying to reposition their product or service so that the intended customers use it in intended ways. This is downright stupid—on a tactical level, take the money! When flowers are blossoming, your task is to see where and why they are blossoming and then adjust your business to reflect this information.

Here are three eye-opening examples of blossoming flowers cited by the dean of entrepreneurial writing, Peter F. Drucker:

- The inventor of Novocain intended it as a replacement for general anesthesia for doctors. Doctors, however, refused to use it and continued to rely upon traditional methods. Dentists, by contrast, quickly adopted it, so the inventor focused on this unforeseen market.

*Found at http://www.anecdotage.com/index.php?aid=14700.

- Univac was the early leader in computers. However, it considered computers the tool of scientists, so it hesitated to sell its product to the business market. IBM, by contrast, wasn't fixated on scientists and thus let its products blossom as business computers. This is why IBM is a household name, and you can only read about Univac in history books.

- An Indian company bought the license to manufacture a European bicycle with an auxiliary engine. The bicycle wasn't successful, but the company noticed many orders for only the engine. Investigating this strange development, the company found out that the engine was being used to replace hand-operated pumps to irrigate fields. The company went on to sell millions of irrigation pumps.*

The following matrix shows a useful way to think of blossoming flowers. Most companies want to occupy the top left corner. The real action is in the bottom right corner, so be flexible and be open to unforeseen customers and uses.

	INTENDED CUSTOMER	UNINTENDED CUSTOMER
Intended Use	Expected	Delightful (Example: car dealers—not only private owners—selling used cars on eBay)
Unintended Use	Delightful (Example: women using Avon's Skin So Soft as an insect repellent)	Astounding (Example: computer novices creating newsletters, magazines, and forms with Macintoshes)

*Peter F. Drucker, *Innovation and Entrepreneurship: Practice and Principles* (New York: Harper & Row, 1985), 190–91.

SEE THE GORILLA

Daniel J. Simons of the University of Illinois and Christopher F. Chabris of Harvard University ran an interesting experiment that has rainmaking implications. They asked students to watch a video of two teams of players throwing basketballs to one another. The students' task was to count how many passes one team made to their teammates.

Photo credit: A single frame from a video by Daniel Simons and Christopher Chabris. The video is available as a part of the *Surprising Studies of Visual Awareness* DVD from Viscog Productions, Inc. (www.viscog.com). Copyright 2003 by Daniel J. Simons. Used with permission.

Thirty-five seconds into the video, an actor dressed as a gorilla entered the room the players were in, thumped his chest, and remained in the video for another nine seconds. When asked, fifty percent of the students did not notice the gorilla!* Apparently, they were attending to the assigned task of counting passes and were perceptually blind to extraneous events.

The same phenomenon occurs in organizations: Everyone is focused on the intended customers and intended uses, and they fail to see flowers blossoming in unexpected ways. Univac, in the example cited previously, focused on the scientific market and failed to see the

*Michael Shermer, "None So Blind," *Scientific American* (March 2004).

business market—unlike IBM. You must let a hundred flowers blossom *and* pick the unexpected ones—the gorilla markets in the midst, so to speak—to make it rain.

PICK THE RIGHT LEAD GENERATION METHOD

Many entrepreneurs, particularly ones with technical backgrounds, rely on traditional methods of generating sales leads, such as advertising and telemarketing. This reliance tends to be reinforced if managers with "proven backgrounds" from large companies join the team.

These methods might work if people *bought* the products and services of startups. However, recall that the products and services of startups are *sold*, not bought. For selling to work, entrepreneurs need to establish their credibility and develop face-to-face, personalized contact—an effort that begins with effective lead generation.

Henry DeVries of the New Client Marketing Institute investigated methods of generating leads. He found that the most effective technique was conducting small-scale seminars to introduce the product— not advertising, telemarketing, making glossy brochures, or exhibiting at trade shows. These are his top five methods:

1. Conducting small-scale seminars
2. Giving speeches
3. Getting published
4. Networking in a proactive way
5. Participating in industry organizations

It's risky to generalize his findings to every business, but they do contradict traditional thinking, and you should consider them when you're trying to make it rain.

FIND THE KEY INFLUENCER

"Data base administrator III." This sounds like an unlikely title for a decision maker. It conjures a picture of someone stuffed in a messy cubicle jammed full of technical manuals, eating Subway sandwiches for lunch.

Lisa Nirell was a rainmaker at BMC Software. One such data base administrator III (DBAIII) bought more than $400,000 worth of software from her company. Stuck in his cubicle, phone constantly ringing, this DBAIII influenced the major purchases for his company. When the executive vice president had questions about projects or vendors, it was Mr. DBAIII he visited.

The higher you go in big companies, the thinner the oxygen; and the thinner the oxygen, the more difficult it is to support intelligent life. Thus, intelligence is concentrated in the middles and bottoms of large companies. Here is a key insight for rainmakers:

Ignore titles and find the true key influencers.

Logically, the next question is "How do I find out who the key people are and get to them?" The answer is that you have to ask secretaries, administrative aides, and receptionists—which leads us to the next point: Suck down.

SUCK DOWN

I've made dozens of decisions about companies and people by consulting two terrific assistants at Apple and at Garage: Carol Ballard and Holly Lory. I would ask them such questions as "What do you think of that guy?" or "What do you think of this idea?" If their answers were "He's a jerk," "He's rude," "He's an egomaniac," or "It's a dumb idea," he or it was finished with us.

You may think it astounding that assistants had such power and influence with me—*Surely Guy is the exception to the rule. In most cases, executives carefully consider every phone call, meeting, and e-mail and then tell an assistant what to do.* Dream on. What I've described is how the world works.

Rainmaking requires access to your key influencers and decision makers. This includes face-to-face access, telephone access, or even e-mail access. Unfortunately, these kinds of people are bombarded by salespeople—every one of them with a "great" product or service. (No one ever calls to sell a piece of crap.)

Hence, many key influencers and decision makers employ people to shield them from rainmakers. Let's call them "umbrellas." To make it rain, you have to learn how to suck down to umbrellas. They are called secretaries, administrative aides, and sometimes even data base administrators III. Sucking up is vastly overrated—sucking up cannot work unless you first get through the phalanx of umbrellas, so read on to learn how to effectively suck down.

- **UNDERSTAND THEM.** You may think that their job is to prevent you from gaining access. Don't flatter yourself. You're not that important. Their job is to enable the executive to do his job—and one aspect of this is guarding his time (which many people, such as you, might waste).

- **DON'T TRY TO BUY THEM.** No one likes to be bought—or, more accurately, to be thought of as someone who could be bought—so don't send gifts to bribe your way in. The way to get in is to have a credible introduction and a rock-solid proposition and then to treat every contact in the organization with respect and civility.

  After you've had access (whether the access worked out or not), you can follow up with an e-mail, handwritten note, or gift. Sometimes the most effective follow-up is a photocopy of an article the umbrella would find interesting. Whatever you do, gratitude is always better than bribery.

- **EMPATHIZE WITH THEM.** Odds are, this person isn't making much money—certainly a pittance compared to the executive. And the umbrella could probably run the place better than the executive. Companies pay umbrellas small salaries, so don't think they "should" take your abuse.

- **NEVER COMPLAIN ABOUT THEM.** Even if the umbrella is stone-cold wrong, never go over his head and complain. The first thing that will happen is that this complaint will circle back to the umbrella, and you can kiss your access goodbye. Forever.

GO AFTER AGNOSTICS, NOT ATHEISTS

[T]he defenders of traditional theory and procedure can almost always point to problems that its new rival has not solved but that for their view are no problems at all. *

—Thomas Kuhn

One of the holy grails of rainmaking is landing "the reference account." This is the big, prestigious account that provides wheelbarrows of money, plus credibility, too.

Back in the mid-eighties, the reference-account software companies for a new personal computer were Ashton-Tate (dBase) and Lotus Development (Lotus 123). Oh, to have their products run on Macintosh . . . it would establish Macintosh as viable. But it was not to be—and it didn't matter.

By definition, reference accounts are already successful and established. Usually, they benefit from the perpetuation of the status quo. Herein lies the problem: If you have an innovative product or service, these accounts are the least likely to embrace it. They are atheists when it comes to a new religion because they are the high priests of an old order.

Unfortunately, many startup organizations obsess about landing these reference accounts—as Apple did with Ashton-Tate and Lotus. They will do almost anything to have them as customers because their presence is the equivalent of being blessed by the Pope.

Take it from someone who did it wrong: Ignore atheists. Look instead for agnostics—people who don't deny your religion and who are at least willing to consider the existence of your product or service. If your dream reference account doesn't "get it," cut your losses and move on.

Agnostics, or "nonconsumers,"† typically aren't using anything because of the high cost or skill requirements of the current offerings.

---

*Thomas Kuhn, *The Structure of Scientific Revolutions* (Chicago: University of Chicago Press, 1962), 157.

†Clayton Christensen and Michael E. Raynor, *The Innovator's Solution* (Boston: Harvard Business School Press, 2003), 110–11.

For example, during the introductory phase of personal computers in the eighties, people couldn't afford personal mainframes or minicomputers. Even if they could, these products were so hard to use that consumers wouldn't have had the necessary skill level.

Thus, agnostics are easier to please than atheists because you're enabling them to do something they simply could not do before—as opposed to having to displace an entrenched product or service. Apple seldom got people to switch from Windows (despite its ad campaign), but for people who had never used a personal computer before, Macintosh was life-changing.

Nothing should excite an entrepreneur more than penetrating a market full of agnostics.

MAKE PROSPECTS TALK

Nature, which gave us two eyes to see and two ears to hear, has given us but one tongue to speak.

—Jonathan Swift

If a sales prospect is willing to buy your product or service, he will often tell you what it will take to close the deal. All you have to do is shut up so your prospects can talk.

The process is simple: (a) create a comfortable environment by asking permission to ask questions, (b) ask questions, (c) listen to the answers, (d) take notes, and (e) explain how your product or service fills their needs—but only if it does. And yet many people fail at this:

- They are not prepared to ask good questions. It takes research before a meeting to understand a prospect. Furthermore, they are afraid that asking questions makes it look as if they don't already know the answer.

- They can't shut up because they belong to the bludgeon school of sales: I'll keep talking until the prospect submits and agrees to buy. Or, they may be able to shut up, but then they don't bother listening. (Hearing is involuntary; listening is not.)

- They don't take notes because they are lazy or don't consider the information important. Taking notes is a good idea, as mentioned in Chapter 7, "The Art of Raising Capital." First, it will help you remember things. Second, it's bound to impress the prospect that you care enough about what was said to write it down.

- They don't know enough about their product or service to effectively apply it to the needs of prospects. This is inexcusable.

Let's say that your product offers several different benefits (not features!) such as saving money, providing peace of mind, and enlightening people. Begin by mentioning all three benefits and let prospects react. They will typically tell you which of the benefits are appealing.

If nothing resonates, ask the prospect what would. From that point on, focus on what you just heard because the prospect has just offered you a valuable tidbit: "This is how to sell to me." The point is to let the prospect talk, to listen, and then to be flexible. Remember: You're selling, they aren't necessarily buying. If a customer tells you how to sell to them, you damn well better listen.

ENABLE TEST DRIVES

The most difficult barrier that startups face is reliance on the status quo. Usually people think the old products and services are good enough: *I can do everything I want to with my computer with a text-based interface. Why would I want a graphical user interface?*

This doesn't mean that every product in widespread use is good enough—only that customers have accepted them as such. Thus, an entrepreneur's job is often to show people why they need something new. The traditional way to do this is to bludgeon them with advertising and promotion.

However, countless companies have already flooded the marketplace with the same claim: better, faster, cheaper! Also, as a new organization, you probably don't have enough money to reach critical mass in advertising and promotion.

Thus, the best way for a startup to attract customers is to enable them to test drive its product or service. Basically, you are saying

- "We think you're smart." (This already sets you apart from most organizations.)
- "We won't try to bludgeon you into becoming a customer."
- "Please test drive our product or service."
- "Then you decide."

Test driving is different for every business. Here are some examples that illustrate widespread applicability:

- H. J. Heinz (2002 revenues of $9.4 billion) gave away samples of his pickles at the 1893 Chicago World's Fair. His booth was stuck in a low-traffic location, so he hired kids to pass out tickets that promised a free souvenir for visiting his booth to get a pickle.*

- General Motors created the GM 24-Hour Test Drive program to enable people to take cars home for the evening in order to truly test drive them. This sure beats the usual car-dealership test drive of going around the block.

- Salesforce.com enabled people to use its software for a thirty-day period at no charge. The beauty of this test drive is that once you have this kind of information about a company's product, you're less likely to switch because of the data entry you've already done.

Suspend your dependence on traditional and expensive methods of marketing your product or service and give test driving a test drive. It's the best way to overcome the status quo.

PROVIDE A SAFE, EASY FIRST STEP

One of the mistakes Apple made when we introduced Macintosh was that we asked information technology managers to throw out existing

*Maggie Overfelt, "A World (Fair) of Invention," *Fortune Small Business* (April 2003): 31.

computers and replace them with Macintoshes. We were asking them to take a leap of faith. With hindsight, it should not have been surprising that few companies took us up on this request.

Mixing metaphors, if you want to make it rain, don't try to boil the ocean. Instead, offer customers a smooth, gentle, and slippery adoption curve. This means asking customers to use your product or service in small pieces of the business, in a limited and low-risk manner:

- one geographic location, such as a regional office
- one department or function
- one project
- a brief trial period
- a simple act of support

Assuming that you do have a great product or service, simply getting in the door is the hardest part of the battle. If you're lucky, your product or service will please the customer, and satisfaction will catalyze further adoption. It seldom goes this smoothly, however, because while getting it in is hard, getting it used is just as hard, as is getting it spread. But the process always starts with getting it in.

Counterintuitive as this may seem, you should also implement a safe, easy *last* step for customers—that is, to make it easy for customers to end their relationship with you. For example, Netflix, the DVD subscription service, has an easy and friendly five-minute process to end subscription to its service. It enables people to have a positive last experience with the company.

It's far better for former customers to say, "Netflix wasn't for me because I don't watch that many DVDs," than "It took me an hour on the phone and three months of fighting with my credit card company before I could unsubscribe. I will never use Netflix again."

Furthermore, because of the good feelings that Netflix's exit procedure generates, former customers are much more willing to reinstate their accounts when they receive Netflix's friendly e-mails a few weeks later.

LEARN FROM REJECTION

If you're not part of the solution, you're part of the precipitate.
—Henry J. Tillman

Rainmakers get rejected. In fact, the best rainmakers probably get rejected more often because they are making more pitches than others. However, a good rainmaker learns two lessons from rejection: first, how to improve his rainmaking; second, what kind of prospects to avoid. Here is a list of the most common rejections and what to learn from them:

- **"YOU ARE NOT ONE OF US. STOP TRYING TO BE ONE OF US."** You typically encounter this rejection when you are trying to change fundamentally how something is done. For example, when Apple introduced the Macintosh, Apple attempted (and failed) to gain acceptance by selling Macintoshes to information technology departments. When people tell you this, go around or under them. For example, selling Macintoshes to the graphics department worked for Apple.

- **"YOU DON'T HAVE YOUR ACT TOGETHER."** One of two things happened: Either you really didn't have your act together or you stepped on someone's toes. Force yourself to review your pitch and interpersonal skills to determine if it's the former. If you stepped on someone's toes, figure out how to make amends.

- **"YOU ARE INCOMPREHENSIBLE."** You usually hear this when you are, in fact, incomprehensible. Go back to the basics: Cut out the jargon, redo your pitch from scratch, and practice your pitch. The burden of proof is upon you—if you need to find a customer who's "smart enough to understand why they need our product," you're going to starve to death.

- **"YOU ARE ASKING US TO CHANGE, AND WE DON'T WANT TO HEAR THIS."** This is a common response when presenting to a successful group that is living the high life and sees no reason to change. What you're hearing is that you're in the right market but talking to the wrong customers, so look for customers who are feeling pain.

- **"YOU ARE A SOLUTION LOOKING FOR A PROBLEM."** This means that you are still inside your value proposition looking out. The appropriate response is to keep permutating your value proposition until you are outside the value proposition (like customers) and looking in. If you can't get on the outside, let's face it: You may, in fact, be a solution looking for a problem.

- **"WE'VE DECIDED TO STANDARDIZE ON ANOTHER PRODUCT (OR SERVICE)."** You're probably trying to sell to the wrong person if you hear this and your product or service is truly, demonstrably better. Avoid the gatekeeper and find the user. Do what you have to do to get an entrée to the final customer. If your product or service isn't truly, demonstrably better, maybe the final customer told the gatekeeper to get rid of you.

MANAGE THE RAINMAKING PROCESS

Rainmaking is a process, not a one-time event or an act of God. You can't abdicate it to some "sales types" or to sheer luck. It is a process; you can manage it like other processes in your organization. Here are some tips for how to do this:

- **ENCOURAGE EVERYONE TO MAKE IT RAIN.** Someday you may reach the point where your engineers and inventors can simply toss a new product or service over the cubicle wall and have the salespeople pick it up and sell it. But that day isn't here yet.

- **SET GOALS FOR SPECIFIC ACCOUNTS:** when you expect them to close, and how much each sale will yield on a weekly, monthly, and quarterly basis.

- **TRACK LEADING INDICATORS.** Everyone has trailing indicators, such as the previous month's and quarter's sales. Leading indicators, such as the number of new product ideas, cold calls, or sales leads, are important, too. It's easy to know where you've been—it's harder and more valuable to know where you're going.

- **RECOGNIZE AND REWARD TRUE ACHIEVEMENTS.** Don't allow rainmakers to submit intentionally low forecasts so that they can easily beat them. Certainly don't recognize and reward intentions— intentions are easy, rainmaking is hard.

If you don't manage the rainmaking process, you'll start with "Our projections are conservative," and six months later, you'll be saying, "Our sales are coming in slower than expected." There is nothing sadder.

FAQ

Q. Where would I find the early adopters and risk takers in large companies?

A. It's difficult to provide a general answer to this question. It's easier to tell you where you probably *won't* find these types of people: at the highest levels. So let a hundred flowers blossom inside these companies—don't go in with preconceived notions of who the early adopters are.

Q. We have the opportunity to hire a rainmaker, but he wants significant stock options, plus $150,000 per year, plus another $75,000 in expense accounts. That's in addition to our trade show and advertising budget. He's got a good reputation and accounted for $16 million per year in sales in his previous job and says this will be a big step down in terms of income. Why should we hire him rather than going with manufacturers' representatives?

A. Rainmakers are expensive, but if they can deliver, they're worth it. If he wants the world—and it sounds like that's the case in this scenario—make him earn it with a compensation plan dependent upon results. I wouldn't simply give him everything he wants at the start.

RECOMMENDED READING

Cialdini, Robert. *Influence: The Psychology of Persuasion*. New York: Morrow, 1993.

Coleman, Robert E. *The Master Plan of Evangelism*. Grand Rapids, MI: Spire Books, 1994.

Moore, Geoffrey. *Crossing the Chasm: Marketing and Selling High-Tech Products to Mainstream Customers*. New York: Harper Business, 1999.

Obligation

CHAPTER 11

The Art of Being a Mensch

The true measure of a man is how he treats someone who can do him absolutely no good.
—Samuel Johnson

GIST

T his chapter explains how to achieve menschhood. *Mensch* is the Yiddish term for a person who is ethical, decent, and admirable. It is the highest form of praise one can receive from the people whose opinions matter.

This topic is included here for two reasons:

- Every person and organization exists in the larger context of society. Doing things that benefit you and your organization to the detriment of the rest of society doesn't scale.
- If you want to build a truly great, lasting organization, you need to set the highest moral and ethical standards for employees. A mensch, by definition, provides a good role model for this.

The three foundations of menschhood are helping lots of people, doing what's right, and paying back society—simple concepts that are hard to implement.

HELP MANY PEOPLE

Getting into Heaven may require the simple act of accepting God, but according to some theories, there are different "classes" in Heaven once you get there. Let's call these tiers (for want of a better analogy) coach, business, and first class. (Heaven may not work this way, but we're talking about eternity, so why take any chances?)

As in airplane travel, the salient issue is *How do I get upgraded?* You have to rack up points through your conduct during the time you're on this earth, and the best way to rack up points is to help people.

The easiest people to help are those whom you think you'll need someday. Unfortunately, these points are the least valuable because the motivation isn't pure. Many people don't even bother doing this.

The big points, and what separates a mensch from a good schemer, come from helping people who cannot help you. In ascending order of karmic purity, there are three reasons to help these folks:

- You never know—they might be able to help you someday.
- You want to be sure to rack up karmic points just in case my theories are right.
- You derive intrinsic joy from helping your fellow man.

The first reason will get you into an exit row in coach class. The second will get you into business class. The third will get you into first class on Singapore Airlines in a seat that converts to a fully reclining bed with a power outlet for your laptop and noise-canceling headphones on a plane with in-flight Internet access.

But let's not get caught up in details. A mensch helps people regardless of whether it's good for this life or the next one. There are few joys greater than helping others.

DO WHAT'S RIGHT

Doing what's right is the second cornerstone of menschhood. This means taking the high, and sometimes difficult, road. Here are three examples:

- **OBSERVE THE SPIRIT OF AGREEMENTS.** An investment bank finds a buyer for your company, helps you negotiate an acceptable price, and finalizes the deal. However, the deal closes a month after the engagement agreement expires, and the fee that you would receive is $500,000. You pay the bank anyway. Gladly.

- **PAY FOR WHAT YOU GET.** You're a jewelry retailer, and you've received a shipment of rings from a manufacturer. The manufacturer billed you for fourteen-carat gold, but they are eighteen-karat rings. You call the manufacturer and report the discrepancy.

- **FOCUS ON WHAT'S IMPORTANT.** You're in a beginner's hockey league. At midseason, your team is 8–0. The next-best team is 4–4; the worst team is 0–8. Some of your best players offer to swap places with players on the last-place team.* What's important is for everyone to have fun, not winning the championship.

A mensch does the right thing—not the easy thing, the expedient thing, the money-saving thing, or the I-can-get-away-with-it thing. Right is right, and wrong is wrong. There absolutely are absolutes in life, and mensches heed and exemplify this truth.

PAY BACK SOCIETY

The third cornerstone of menschhood is paying back society. You could define a mensch as an investor who doesn't care about capital gains. The kind of gains a mensch does seek is paying back society, not reaping additional money.

This doesn't mean that a mensch has to be wealthy. In fact, money usually renders a person unmenschionable. (If you ever want to understand what God thinks of money, look at who He gives it to.)

---

*And just to show you how the karmic scoreboard works, the last-place team wins the championship at the end of the season.

A mensch wants to pay back society for the following kinds of gifts:

- family and friends
- spiritual fulfillment
- good health
- beautiful surroundings
- economic success
- a hat trick every once in a while

There are many "currencies" to use to pay back society. Giving money is only one of them—others include giving time, expertise, and emotional support. Mensches joyfully provide these currencies to others. The key concept is that a mensch pays *back*—that is, for goodness already received—as opposed to pays *forward* in expectation of return.

EXERCISE

It is the end of your life. Write down the three things you want people to remember about you:

1.

2.

3.

FAQ

Q. How can I prevent success from going to my head?

A. Death and illness have had a profound effect on me in this regard. Neither cares whether you're rich, famous, or powerful. And all the riches, fame, and power don't matter if you're sick or dead. So when you're feeling invincible, just remember that you could be gone in a split second, and "richest person in the hospital" and "richest person in the cemetery" are lousy positioning statements.

Q. How can I make sales calls and close business deals without always feeling like I "pulled one over on" the customer?

A. If you're selling something that the customer needs, you should never feel this way. If you do feel this way, stop selling what you're selling— or sell it to people who need it.

Q. Isn't thinking of others and being charitable antithetical to the goal of business—that is, to make money? Won't a potential investor see this as a sign of someone who is soft or weak or otherwise not an effective business-person?

A. If a potential investor feels this way, it says more about the investor than it says about you. It's entirely possible to do good and make good. The two are not mutually exclusive. However, don't assume that your charitable causes are the same as your investors'. And you should be charitable with your own resources, not someone else's.

Q. What if otherwise helpful and positive me really needs to lash out at someone?

A. This is what an ice rink is for—although I've been known to lash out off (and on) the ice a few times myself. (It made the situations worse.) As I've gotten older, I've learned to shut up (or not send the e-mail) and walk away.

Q. People are always asking me for my expert advice, but it's interfering with my ability to get my current job done. What should I do?

A. Write a book and tell everyone to buy it.

RECOMMENDED READING

Halberstam, Joshua. *Everyday Ethics: Inspired Solutions to Real-Life Dilemmas.* New York: Viking, 1993.

Afterword

Books are good enough in their own way, but they
are a mighty bloodless substitute for living.
—Robert Louis Stevenson

Thank you for reading my book. This took an investment of both your time and your money. In return, I hope that you have gained insight into how to make meaning and change the world.

I also hope to meet you someday. If you have the book with you, you can show me how you took notes, dog-eared pages, and underlined text. Nothing is more flattering to an author than to see that his book is severely "used."

From time to time, please check www.artofthestart.com, because I will upload examples, templates, and other resources for your use.

Now I've kept you too long. Cast away the microscopes, focus the telescopes, and get going.

Guy Kawasaki
Palo Alto, California
Kawasaki@garage.com

Index

Invariably, the best scholarly indexes are made by authors who have the ability to be objective about their work, who understand what a good index is, and who have mastered the mechanics of the indexing craft.

—The Chicago Manual of Style